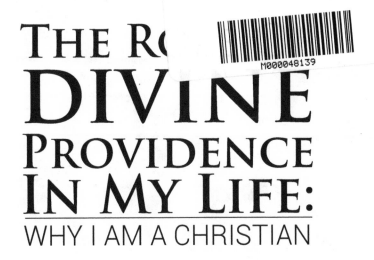

THE RO
DIVINE
PROVIDENCE
IN MY LIFE:
WHY I AM A CHRISTIAN

CHIA ALPHONSE TASAH

Printed in the United States of America

Library of Congress Control Number: 2020905334
ISBN:Softcover   9781643769349
eBook   1643769332

Republished by: PageTurner Press and Media LLC
Publication Date: 03/19/2020

To order copies of this book, contact:

PageTurner Press and Media
Phone: 1-888-447-9651
order@pageturner.us
www.pageturner.us

To my courageous kids, Kaemia Chia Tasah and Alan Tasah, who were upbeat and readily available to help despite the traumatic impact of my illness on them. They supported God's interworking toward the miraculous recovery from my ailments.

Acknowledgments

I am indebted to my immediate family and all the churches and social groups that prayed to help me earn the blessings that God has bestowed upon me.

I am also grateful for the encouragement and comfort of my wife, BiyohTawa, and my children, Kaemia Chia Tasah and Alan Tasah, who fought tooth and nail during my illness to get me back to my normal self. I am grateful for the Cameroonian community in Minnesota, especially the Kom and Nkambe tribal meetings, for all their support through prayers.

All my appreciation goes to Mr. Alan Lakomski, Mr. Bill Strassberger, and Dr. Christine Swanson for accepting God into my life as my stepping-stone into a better version of myself

Finally I beg the forgiveness of all those who have been with me over the course of the years whose names I have failed to mention.

Preface

This book, *The Role of Divine Providence in My Life: Why I Am a Christian*, typifies God's incomprehensible love toward me from conception to adulthood through his grace on my plans for all my tomorrow. God bestowed blessings upon me by stepping into my destiny through an orchestration of happenstances that transformed my life. I believe that my livelihood is inherent in divine providence, exemplified by my death and resurrection that I wish to share with you.

When I wrote *The Life of an African Peace Corps Child*, a text that recounts my childhood transition into adulthood, I reflected on my journey from early life into adulthood and discernibly believed that a supernatural force steered my fortune. I thought that divine providential interventions made me a better version of myself.

Cameroon is located in poverty-stricken sub-Saharan Africa, which to me was a divine blessing. Being a Cameroonian was fateful because I was poverty-stricken, and poverty revolved around my destiny in point and time. God fortuitously intervened to steer my fortune by masterminding fateful coincidences that directed motion favorably as I progressed in life. Each human has his or her choices and priorities that influences his or her destiny per God's design.

God inserted himself into almost all my endeavors by transforming mishaps into celebratory achievements. If I missed one step, my story would never be mine. In this regard, a supernatural force constructed coincidences of events that moved me forward in a quest for a better life despite unprivileged background, showcased by my father's reluctance to work. His state of poverty infected the whole family and I became a victim of circumstance by Gods grace. Poverty noted to ridicule ones status in society propitiously elevated my status in my community/.

The bartender job I worked in the backdrop of poverty fatefully earned a Peace Corps benefactor, Mr. Alan Lakomski, who sympathized with my neediness and sponsored my secondary education when I was fifteen. Alan was an epitome of hope who set precedence on benevolent gestures and allowed destiny to take its course. When he left unexpectedly, another heaven-sent Peace Corps volunteer, Bobe Bill Strassberger, reentered my life when I faced the ordeal of dropping out of school, an occurrence I detested without any alternative on the horizon for obvious reasons. He inculcated self-reliant skills, and I was able to support my education without any stand-alone sponsor.

When I struggled through insurmountable difficulties at the University of Buea, I luckily connected with the most solicitous and hospitable Peace Corps benefactor, Dr. Christine Swanson, who supervised my end-of-course project. Divine providence randomly placed me under her supervision of my end-of-course project, one of the five she oversaw. We became close friends in Buea, Cameroon, and as returned Peace Corps workers living in Minnesota.

Upon request, she encouraged me to apply to the University of Minnesota and supported my visa process until I got it. Upon my arrival to the United States, she provided negotiated lodging in her neighbor's condo when all my relatives and friends from Cameroon declined to take responsibility. As a temporary dweller under her supervision, : I was lucky to reconnect with my original Peace Corps sponsors, Mr. Alan Lakomski and Bobe Bill Strassberger who were helpful in Cameroon. They forestalled the ordeal of homelessness and/or deportation because I was desperate financially with no feeding and lodging needs. Both readily accepted and supported me, as they had done for twenty-three years from 1980 in Cameroon.

Bobe Bill Strassberger educated me on American culture, and Alan Lakomski forestalled the threat of homelessness by providing me with financial support. I now hold a master of education degree in human resource development (MEd) and am married with two kids.

In 2006 I got a job as a parking services specialist at Fairview South Dale Hospital in Edina, Minnesota, and worked passionately and ethically but was wrongfully discharged on June 7, 2013, for flimsy reasons. Depression caused by the trauma from wrongful termination kicked in. I encountered a traumatic illness from memory lapses that almost took my life. An immune system disorder and eventual breakdown of my nervous system compounded my ailments. The immune system disorder ravaged almost all my white blood cells, reducing them to just one. A medical student indicated I was lucky because immunosuppression might also be deliberately induced with drugs, as in preparation for bone marrow or other organ transplantation, to prevent the rejection of a transplant, but mine just occurred.

What happened to me is incomprehensible and unexplainable because God is the most talented doctor. I reportedly died for a few minutes and was restored back to life. I believe it was God's intervention to resurrect me in order to testify his goodness in my entire life to the world.

The minute I descended into death, like Jesus, God loved me, took hold, and held me back up. I now drive after a two-year restriction and a rigorous driving assessment and testing. I published a book, *The Life of an African Peace Corps Child* and am now working on *The Role of Divine Providence in My Life: Why I Am a Christian*. I'm most proud of the blessings that God has bestowed upon me in my life. He's given me the vision to truly see that you can fall down but still get back up by God's grace. I thank God every day of my life through prayers to renew my strength and courage to move forward.

Introduction

According to Merriam-Webster dictionary, divine providence is the foreseeing care and guidance of God or nature over the creatures of the earth. It is also conceived as the power sustaining and guiding human destiny. Traditional theism holds that God is the creator of heaven and earth and all that occurs in the universe takes place under divine providence, that is, under God's sovereign guidance and control. According to believers, God governs creation as a loving father, working all things for good.

This book depicts God's interworking in my life via his extraordinary intervention in my existence. "For I know the plans I have for you, declares the Lord, plans for welfare and not for evil, to give you a future and a hope" (Jer. 29:11 ESV).

Ocular Proof of Divine Providence

A clear case of divine providence overriding sin is the story of Judas Iscariot, whom God allowed to lie, deceive, cheat, steal, and finally betray the Lord Jesus into the hands of his enemies. All of this was a great wickedness, and God was displeased. Yet at the same time, all of Judas's plotting and scheming led to a greater good, humankind's salvation. Jesus had to die at the Romans' hands to become the sacrifice for sin. If Jesus had not been crucified, we would still be in our sins.

But how did God get Christ to the cross? He providentially allowed Judas the freedom to perform a series of wicked acts. Jesus plainly states in Luke 22:22 (NIV), "The Son of Man will go as it has been decreed. But woe to that man who betrays him!"

Imagine something happening exactly when needed without any foreplan and creates a positive impact in your life. God knows and sees everything, and he knows you know better than you know yourself. He can do everything and loves you. Things have happened in my life without any foreplaning and accelerated my growth process. This is why I felt the need to testify the goodness of God. Despite the hardship and pitfalls I encountered in my developmental process, my ultimate motivation that ignited into determination is God. I cast myself at his feet so he might renew my strength and provide courage each day of my life while I rest in his presence. He has worked everything for the good of those who love him, especially his inner workings in me. Providence means you don't have to worry or fret. A God larger than you has it under control.

Divine Providence In The Story Of Joseph

In the book of Genesis, we can see God's providence on display in the life of Joseph. Jacob, the grandson of Abraham, had 12 sons, of which Joseph was the 11th and had been the favorite of his father, expressed through the gift of a multicolored robe given by Jacob to his son (Genesis 37:3). With the onset of jealousy, Jacob's brothers, except the youngest Benjamin, sold him into slavery which ultimately led him into the service of Potipher (Genesis 37:12-36 NIV). After being falsely accused by Potipher's wife, Joseph wound up in prison, but redemption came through the interpretation of several dreams that led him to become (prime minister) second only to Pharaoh in power and authority. Genesis recounts the story of Joseph, multiple times the text states that "the Lord was with Joseph". It would have been easy for him to look at the circumstances that happened and place blame either on his brothers or God. Likewise, it would have been just as easy for Joseph to take credit for working his way up from prison to a position of power and authority. But Joseph recognized that it was not the working of his brothers selling him into slavery and it was not his own doing that elevated him to his status, it was the hand of God working purposely in all things to bring about his will.

Joyce Meyer said, "Jesus is a divine guest inside of you all the time—one who loves, understands, sees and hears you. He wants to live in oneness with you . . . to be the centerpiece of everything you do." http://www.dailyquotes.live/quotes/567676/

When I reflected on the biological composition of my parents, which resulted in me, one of their offspring, I discerned God's extraordinary interventions in my life and procreation at large. In the conception of a human person, God creates an entirely new human soul that a factory cannot produce because of a complicated anatomy that is unperceived by humans except those trained scientifically. The characteristic peculiarities and technicalities of something like the human body is difficult to grasp, making the inner workings of God on procreation a huge mystery.

> So God created man in his own image, in the image of God he created him; male and female he created them. And God blessed them. And God said to them, "Be fruitful and multiply and fill the earth and subdue it and have dominion over the fish of the sea and over the birds of the heavens and over every living thing that moves on the earth. (Gen. 1:27–28 NKJV)

I was born third in line into a peasant nuclear family, including my father, mother, and nine children. My parents endured poverty because they were uneducated and unqualified to work. My dad relied on his affluent brother, who worked at the Cameroon Development Cooperation (CDC) and died in a ghastly accident on his way to Njinikom, Kom, my village. My father, traumatized by his brother's death, couldn't come to terms with himself why his brother died at the prime of his age. So my father thought he would follow suit.

Despondent, he didn't want to expend restful energy working, so he upheld the notion of anticipated death and decided to not embark on any income-generating activities because work was just a waste. Unfortunately, God prolonged his life, and he died at the age of seventy-five in 1998. This is why we endured protracted poverty.

In anguish of his brother's loss, my father gave up on himself, and we were deprived of basic human needs, leading us into abject poverty. His state of poverty revolved around my developmental process from babyhood to adulthood, and destiny guided my journey. I believe that, from conception, God created me for a purpose and carved out a pathway to my achievements as I worked diligently and aggressively to achieve my utmost goals.

Despite my parents' penury, they inculcated positive values of love, humility, handwork, and determination. Humility and determination molded my goals, and resilience guided my growth process because I didn't give up on my struggles, but I bounced back heroically in adversity. My mom advised me to not be a quitter, "You have to keep working hard, and one day you shall find your voice." My parents also taught me to love my neighbors as myself, to not steal, and to not

1

be jealous. My mother intimated that humility rewards and arrogance hurts when not needed. I guess the aforementioned values earned the admiration of notables who were well-off seniors and Peace Corps workers, who were strangers to me in the beginning and eventually became my sponsors.

God's interworking manifested in the blend of the biological composition of my parents, which produced me with all my attractive and gainful behavioral attributes that guided me up to myself. The timely coincidences in my life made unworkable situations look viable. I gained the privilege of attaining higher education at the University of Buea, Cameroon, and the University of Minnesota, an elusive dream goal that I'd never envisioned accomplishing during my early childhood transition into adulthood. My parents' beggary had ignited into feelings of despair, and I didn't foresee a pleasurable livelihood. I believe, through God's interworking, destiny conducted me to my destination.

And this explains why I am a practicing Christian.

Chapter 1

Background to My Fortune

Cameroon, My Place of Origin:
The Fateful Location of Cameroon

This Central African country is located north of the Gulf of Guinea (Atlantic Ocean). Its western border is Nigeria. Its southern border is Congo (Brazzaville), Gabon, and Equatorial Guinea. Its eastern border is the Central African Republic. Its northeastern border is Chad. And to the north is Lake Chad.

The Location of Kom Fondom (My Tribe): Fateful

The fondom (chieftain) of Kom is located in Bamenda Grasslands in the present-day northwest region of Cameroon. A fon is the ruler. It is the second largest fondom, after Nso, in the grasslands (Chilver and Kaberry 1967, 33). Kom shares its eastern boundary with the kingdoms of Oku and Nso and the southern frontier with Kedjom Keku, or Big Babanki, and the Ndop Plain. Bafut is on the western border, while to the north are Bum and Mmen. The capital of Kom is Laikom, the seat of the ruler, the fon. Advisors, the Kwifon (supreme traditional council), assist the fon in his administrative duties.

Cameroon, located in sub-Saharan Africa, is one of the poorest regions in the world. According to the Human Development Report, 80 percent of sub-Saharan Africa falls within the "low development" measure on the United Nations human development scale, with an average of gross domestic product per capita of $1,690 USD, one-twentieth that of the United States (Fukuda-Parr 2000).

Rapid population growth, political dictatorships, exploitation by wealthy countries, corruption, droughts, and huge bureaucracies have caused sub-Saharan countries to become even poorer over the past twenty years. According to Hassert and Shapiro (2003), the hardship in most of sub-Saharan Africa has been exacerbated by the agricultural policies of Europe and the United States that have continually subsidized Western farmers to produce excess crops and the accompanying tariffs, which effectively block export of African agricultural products. We believe that everyone should have access to clean water and proper nutrition and should be able to live healthy lives free from preventable diseases like malaria or parasitic infections, but Cameroon does not.

Most families in the rural areas, especially Kom, my tribe, are poverty-stricken, and incomes are low. Most indigenes experience malnutrition, sickness, and limited education opportunities. In Cameroon, especially Kom, the infant mortality rate remains especially high. Statistics show that about 11 percent of newborns are moderately or severely underweight. With limited vaccination coverage each year, Cameroonian children fall ill or die from malaria, malnutrition, and diarrhea.

When we studied in primary school, I used lanterns. It was expensive to manage lanterns because kerosene was needed. That required buying with money, which of course was rarely available. In situations of extreme kerosene need during the test or exam season, I used candles and sometimes moonlight when the sky was clear in the dry season. I was compelled to participate in child labor because my dad was indigent and couldn't sponsor my secondary education. His privation was fateful because his inability to support my schooling was conducted by destiny to leverage me to a different destination. He hoped that, as a bartender, I would earn some revenue from my job to support my education at the start of the next academic year.

By divine design, my dad encouraged me to work as bartender in my village, Njinikom Kom. By divine coincidence, I accepted because I didn't want to be a village loafer. I had come to terms with myself that I needed to procure my needs and support payment for my fees during the next academic year. This was the beginning of my child labor experience at age fourteen. Yet God sent the Peace Corps, and it changed my life.

Being Cameroonian Was a Blessing

As aforementioned, Cameroon, located in sub-Saharan African, is one of the poorest regions in the world. Being a Cameroonian was fateful because I was poor, and poverty revolved around my destiny. God had a plan for me because Jesus is a divine guest inside of you all the time, one who loves, understands, sees, and hears you. God knows and sees everything, and he knows us better than we know ourselves. He can do everything and loves us!

He knew my goals guided me toward achieving them. He gave me the ability to become a productive and caring individual who learned how to forgive, even in the face of destructive forces that loomed over my life, trying to destroy any chances of a normal existence. I rose above the circumstances that tormented and maimed me for years. God stepped into my future of blessings that I could never fantasize as reality. By constantly praying the Holy Rosary and the Chaplet of Diving Mercy, God has bestowed a lot on me, especially what was lacking or robbed from me in my childhood and teenage years.

The world around me had marked me as a child without a future, and some sarcastically derogated me with statements like that. Nonetheless God stepped into my upside-down world and turned my life right side up into a life of serving him and sharing all he offers to culture an assertive belief in him. My testimony of God's miracles in my life might convert doubtful Christians whose faith is weak and cause them to believe that God lives in us. And so they will believe in him.

Only God and you can ascertain your future. He has made my life what it is. Don't ever let anyone dictate or determine your future or tell you that you will not amount to anything in this world. I went from being a bartender out of desperation to a master of education (MEd) student in human resources development from the renowned University of Minnesota, which translated into an honorable degree. It showcases God's extraordinary interventions in my life.

My developmental process from babyhood to adulthood has been impacted by fortuitous coincidences that can be called mysteries of the unknown. Incidental coincidences directed my destiny, and I made headway in life by achieving my utmost goals. I believe that each human has his or her potentials and priorities in life per God's design, and fortune influences every situation, good or bad.

I was born in 1968 in Tinifoinbi, Njinikom, Cameroon. Being a Cameroonian was a means to an end because I was poor, and poverty orbited around my destiny. At first glance, being born into poverty was agonizing, but my relentless struggles to make progress in adversity and hardship turned my pursuits into providential happenstances of numerous achievements. The pathway to my achievements were fraught with obstacles, but by God's grace, I triumphed. If I missed one step, my story wouldn't be mine. In this regard, a supernatural force directed motion toward my achievements in a network of unexplained coincidences that moved me forward despite the pennilessness inherent in our family, showcased by my father's nonchalance feelings toward work.

The Blessing

I was born into a poverty-stricken nuclear family, and our beggary revolved around my destiny. My family's financial situation influenced my job as a bartender at age fourteen, where I providentially earned a pivotal Peace Corps benefactor, Mr. Alan Lakomski, who sympathized with my underprivileged background and sponsored my secondary education at age fourteen, an endeavor my dad was unable to take part in because he was poverty-stricken.

Alan Lakomski, My First Blessing

Alan Lakomski worked as a Peace Corps volunteer in Njinikom, Kom (my tribe). His Peace Corps service was to reorganize the credit union structure in my village of Njinikom and Cameroon at large. One of the credit union offices was in my village Tinifoinbi, directly opposite our homestead. He got to know my living conditions, which might have influenced his sponsorship decision, especially when I mentioned in one of our discussions in the bar that his office in Tinifoinbi was located directly above our homestead. A very empathic and sympathetic man, he favorably impacted my destiny,

When I wrote the first school leaving certificate in 1980 after seven years of primary education and was qualified to attend secondary school, my dad was incapacitated financially by his ailment to support my secondary education. So I stayed at home.

When I kept pestering him to send me to school, my father asked, "Do you want me to squeeze water out of a rock?"

I didn't understand what he meant and asked for an explanation. He said he was very aware of his deteriorated health and lack of a job, and by that, he was penniless. He said he didn't have a few cents to buy his own snuff, and I was hovering around his ears like a mosquito. My proposal to attend an expensive boarding school, like St. Bede's High School Ashing-Kom, baffled him. He didn't want to join in any form of secondary education.

One of our neighbors consented with my parents for me to work as a bartender in a huge bar, all against my will. I hesitated because I had nursed a high propensity for studies and would have loved to continue school instead of serving guests in a bar. I was equally jealous of my friends whom I outsmarted in school academically and otherwise.

At the bar where I worked, there was a private room called confidential where customers who wanted to enjoy their privacy used it, but the decadent downside of the chamber was its obscenities. It was infrequently used as confidential brothel for the owner and some of his colleagues. When the proprietor of the bar lobbied for my services, the thought of working as a bartender was heartbreaking, even though my dad and I didn't have any insight on the job description. I cringed at the notion of working as bartender in a large decadent bar/nightclub that accommodated more than seventy to one hundred customers on weekends. I had heard that inebriated customers caused altercations that led to brawls over girlfriends. Fighting was usually wild with bottles shooting across the sitting area and some slapping on people's heads. Some guests were scarred with deep wounds; others went away unscathed.

I hesitated because I feared being hurt. I had assessed my academic aptitude from my primary school performances and thought I was academically upbeat to embark on a secondary education. I felt I would proceed with my studies, unperturbed by academic failures. In this regard, I was reluctant to work as a bartender, but my dad persisted in his request. So I caved in.

My dad's decision to persist and my change of mind to embrace was fateful because God had a precious gift for me. I was in the loop of direct access connections to a network of unexplained events that propelled me forward. If I rejected that bartender job, I would be languishing in abject poverty today in case I stayed back in my village. I feared that doing a menial job in an obscene, decadent, and hazardous work environment would blunt my growth process. Little did I know that, by God's grace, I would win a sustainable Peace Corps benefactor in Alan Lakomski, who has supported my livelihood struggles until late. I named my son Alan Tasah, derived from Alan Lakomski, to sustain the name legacy.

My dad agreed, and I worked the job as a bartender, starting in 1980. The bar was located at the central roundabout of Njinikom, Kom. It was the only comfortable recreational spot for entertainment and relaxation that welcomed guests from all walks of life. Alan visited the bar infrequently during his breaks to get launch from one grandma who prepared a meal called corn chaff, a mixture of corn and beans boiled and cooked with palm oil. When he ordered his plate, he invited me to eat alongside him. He drank Coca-Cola while I took a Fanta.

During weekends, he came along with other Peace Corps volunteers and Cameroonian friends alike. I treated him courteously, like all others. He was approachable, soft-spoken, and humorous, and he longed to know about the Kom culture and tradition from me. He had a calm and attractive demeanor and asked me frequently why I didn't attend secondary school. He was a down-to-earth person who was interested in learning the Kom culture from me. I did my best to give appropriate answers to the questions he asked about our culture and tradition. What really made us intimate was a traditional game called Fiinjang.

The Game of Fiinjang (Kom)

I had the privilege to become Alan's long-term friend at age fourteen because I played a traditional Kom game called Fiinjang with him. It has a platform of sixteen round holes (houses) with eight holes on either side, and it is played with dark brown seedpods, like round marbles. Each side has eight houses of four seedpods, making thirty-two seedpods on one side. The object of the game is for the winner to move all the seedpods over to his side. It is mostly an adult men's game within Kom, but outside of my tribe, it is a recreational activity in which both genders participate. Women often play, but not in village and subdivisional Fiinjang competitions. Alan learned the game from me, mostly in the morning during his lunch breaks. I had ample time to myself after completing my morning cleaning tasks and sometimes when I had no customers to serve.

A lady called Mami Corn Chaff prepared very palatable corn chaff, that is, corn mixed with beans and spiced, that Alan, Daniel Hunter, and other Peace Corps volunteers loved to eat. When Alan visited the bar for lunch, we sat outside to catch some fresh air. He usually ordered corn chaff, a Fanta for me, and a Coca-Cola for himself. We both enjoyed lunch while playing Fiinjang. I loved corn chaff and ate so much that my friends and classmates nicknamed me "Chaff Chia."

Alan became proficient in the game because of his quick learning skills and outplayed me almost all the time. He laughed at me for failing to catch up with him when I just trained him. My trainee became my trainer. His Fiinjang skills made waves in Njinikom and beyond because he became the most renowned player in our entire village. He participated in the subdivisional Fiinjang competitions with competitors from all over Kom and won.

While playing this game, we consolidated our friendship and became intimate. Alan and I made Fiinjang a conversational game. He sought to learn about my childhood and upbringing, and I longed to know about the United States. He asked why I didn't continue school and burned useful time working as bartender at age fourteen. He intimated that, instead of working as a bartender, I had better further my education so I would be more useful in the future as I grew older.

This is true because I now admire his decision to sponsor my education. If I didn't continue school, I wouldn't be telling my story from the United States. He cautioned that doing a public job like bartending was child abuse in the United States. I told him that my father had a mild stroke that had disabled him, so his disability impeded him to perform in any competitive job. There were no Social Security disability benefits in my country, and we lacked the basic family income for upkeep, let alone going to school.

Alan asked if I aspired to continue school, and I agreed. At the time of our conversation about my plight, three renowned and educated elites of Njinikom were disgusted with my bartender job and hatched plans among themselves to support my education. They were uncomfortable that a good-natured boy with attractive attributes might be corrupted if he indulged in distasteful habits like drugs and all. The elite were the late Francis Nkwain, a member of Parliament under the CNU party; Bobe Chia Kiyam, a retired marketing board worker; and the late Mr. Mbuyongha, then-principal of St. Bede's College, Ashing Kom. They preferred I discontinue my lousy job as a bartender to embark on formal education as my next best alternative.

The aforementioned Kom elite were Alan's friends and spoke positively about me. My dad happened to have been Mr. C. K. Barth's schoolmate. Alan told me that he overheard them debating on who was to take responsibility for my tuition and fees from his table. It was agreed upon that Honorable Francis Nkwain would take responsibility for my fees.

When all the other people left, Alan beckoned me over to his table and asked if his Cameroonian friend who had just left were serious about becoming my secondary school sponsor in charge of paying my fees. He told me that he wanted to help pay my fees if my parents permitted him to so.

To him, he had discerned my modesty from my humble and courteous approach in customer service skills. He pointed out that he could only pay fees for secondary school if my dad and I agreed to procure my needs. According to Alan, my dad was to take care of my school needs, and he would shoulder my tuition and fees. That was his decision, strictly tied to his budget tapped from his meagre Peace Corps volunteer allowance. The game Fiinjang cemented our relationship, and he got to know me better.

In one of our discussions, he intimated that I spoke very good English and exhibited excellent customer service skills that were inherent in smart kids. He thought I would waste my life if I didn't continue school. With that, he was right because I excelled in academics and won academic scholarships as I progressed academically. This is how Alan set precedence in my life through a benevolent gesture and allowed destiny to take its course

When I reflect on the blessings God bestowed upon me during my childhood transition into adulthood, I think of three benevolent Peace Corps volunteers: Alan, Mr. Bill Strassberger, and Dr. Christine Swanson. The only Kom notable (notable owner of a compound) was Bobe C. K. Barth. I believe in God the Father Almighty as professed by the Catholic church by attesting that God's time is the best.

The inception of the Peace Corps program by President John F. Kennedy was divinely inspired by God to transform my life from somewhat destitute to an authentic human, like most well-to-do kids. I believe that extraordinary divine inspiration pushed him into my future.

Role of Fate

Alan's decision was divine intervention. Thoughtful, compassionate, and sympathetic, he conceived the idea of sponsoring my secondary school education. If he didn't send me to school, I would be lost in my village. Fate actually did its work because, without God's mercy by inserting him into my life, I wouldn't have attended school and be a loafer in my village. My dad's decision to endorse the offer for a hazardous job without profound insight about the position's activities was a ploy to keep me busy. My dad and I didn't know the impending luck yet unborn. God positioned a solicitous Peace Corps volunteer, an American stranger named Alan, to set precedence on benevolent gestures toward achieving my foremost education goal. He tested my honesty when he presented 30.000 CFA francs (70 USD) for my school fees for the academic year 1981–1982 in April to pay it in full for September. I paid the fees on the stipulated date on September 15, 1981, and gave him the receipt, and he was happy.

My natural attribute of humility, as derived from my parents and later, earned advice spun around my destiny. I believe the attributes that captured the minds of seniors and Peace Corps volunteers into friendship with me were honesty and humility. I strongly believe these attributes fed their zeal to make me a better version of myself.

Bartender Job Earns the Only Supportive Elite and Notable from My Village

This renowned elite inspired and motivated me toward my education and well-being. My advantageous and/or lucky bartender job propelled me to many achievements. At my job, I made friends with almost all well-off notables of my tribe, uncommon for a young adult's associations. In a typical African village like Njinikom Kom, adults and children, both females and males, do not usually interact on the same platform because family administration is dominated by

11

the man who takes applicable decisions that pertain to all. The most important Kom notable in my life was Bobe C. K. Barth.

When he visited the bar with a number of Kom elite, my customer service skills thrilled him, which urged him to speak positively about me. By God's design, I impressed him by carrying his forty-liter container of gas by headload from the BP gas station near the Njinikom market to his house at Atuilah Njinikom. I didn't know that my humble gesture to help was a powerful personality trait that had a ripple effect upon my life. I had the privilege of becoming his friend.

In Things Fall Apart, Chinua Achebe says, "If a child washed his hands, he could eat with kings." I had just washed my hands, and I was able to interact with a renowned notable. He invited me to his house to help, and I fatefully heeded to his request for home aid and worked exceedingly hard. Fate conducted me to the bar, as you will read in the next paragraphs. I used his personality to get help during my high school studies and beyond.

The bar remains the epicenter of my livelihood. I was planning to scold the proprietor for employing me to work as a bartender at age fourteen, but just realized from my write-ups that the bar was the fulcrum of my livelihood. God chose to position me there against all odds for a reason. The bar jump-started the life I lead now. I thank God for his grace and uplifting.

Bobe C. K. Barth, the president of Kom Bum Development Union, used his influence to give helpful advice to me. Kom Bum Development Union launched a scholarship program to needy, smart, and modest kids during the 1982–1983 academic year. I was qualified in all the requisite requirements and developed a burning eagerness to apply to mitigate my financial problems in school.

I applied for the scholarship and won. The tuition-free scholarship paid all my fees from 1983 to 1986 and catapulted me to my final class in secondary school. I had the privilege of writing and obtaining the General Certificate of Education (GCE) Examination Ordinary Level certificate, a huge impetus to nurse hopes toward a high school education that I had envisioned as illusionary but felt withdrawn to accomplish my higher education dreams for obvious reasons.

Kom notable who was pivotal in connecting me to the Peace Corps by describing my character in detail. Through Alan and Bill, I sat for the GCE. By gaining the privilege of sitting for the secondary school certificate exam, I cultivated the zeal to attend high school without any authentic sponsor but hoped that fate would direct me appropriately. There was no government high school in my village, and I was compelled to study out of my division. It looked very cumbersome to make a high school decision when all my classmates who excelled at the GCE certificate exam were preparing to leave for school.

The good results on the aforementioned exam necessitated the need to show appreciation to the Kom Bum Development Union for lifting the school fee burden from my shoulders by thanking the scholarship board under the auspices of Bobe C. K. Barth. On behalf of the board, he was very impressed with my performance. I was indecisive on either attending the ostentatious Cameroon College of Arts Science and Technology (CCAST) Bambili or Government High School Wum that harnessed cheaper student life because I was realistically upbeat of my financial malaise.

A propitious prompt hinted me to seek advice of sponsorship from Bobe C. K. Barth. He had given me invaluable advice from the time he met me at the bar in 1980 and when I carried his forty-liter container of gas by head from the BP station near the Njinikom market to his house at Atuilah Njinikom. This felicitous gesture connected me intimately with him, and he got to know my parents and me. He pointed out that he was unable to pay for my education and spoke positively but could help in-kind advisably. The scholarship money helped me to save some of the leftovers from Alan and Bill, which helped in the acquisition of basic high school supplies.

His connection to me and the help I got was cumulative because I used his name to gain favors as I grew up. I asked how he could be of help to me at that critical moment. He intimated that he would have been supportive throughout my struggle for continuous education but was just retired and indisposed to help because his pension process was still underway. He had two family friends in Wum and thought he could be of help and any form.

The friends were Mrs. Scott and Ms. Celine Chindo. Ms. Chindo, the vice principal of Government High School, was to help in my admission into high school. Mrs. Scott was to help with my lodging needs in a new subdivision while I sorted out my dwelling place. Both were very close family friends of Mr. C. K. Barth, and he was very positive about their benevolence and ability to help. Mrs. Scott and Ms. Chindo were very gracious and benevolent. Without them, my student life during my first year of high school would have been disruptive and/or wretched. By God's grace, I pushed through life's hurdles and moved forward.

Chapter 2

Second Blessing:
Heaven-Sent Compassionate
Peace Corps Volunteer, Bill Strassberger

When Alan left unexpectedly without a word about my fees, I was unsure and dissolute about getting back to school. It was a torturous predicament ingrained in intrusive thoughts of failure, accompanied by anxiety that led to distractive memories that diverted my attention from self-focus. I wasn't able to think about my overall plight and how to pursue my life goals. This distressing situation was short-lived because a heaven-sent Peace Corps volunteer, Mr. Bill Strassberger, came into my life and chose to support my education. He came in as a fresh Peace Corps worker to replace Dan Hunter. He was to reorganize the Kom Area Cooperative Union to help farmers market their coffee, in collaboration with the Northwest Marketing Board (NWMB). He was to live at the mile thirty-six Wombong (my village) residence. There were no taxis, electricity, and intercity buses.

I fatefully exhibited African hospitality and earned Bill's admiration and sympathy when I co-opted some volunteers to help him by carrying his bags by headloads to his house. As destiny would have it, he became receptive and willing to listen to my story. I tried to mitigate my feelings of anxiety about my schooling impediments through an authentic exposure of my anguish amid fears of becoming a school dropout by recounting my tribulations to Bill. He listened empathically, as his demeanor portrayed. I told him I was distraught and frustrated because my predicament was gut-wrenching, pointing to the fact that I abhorred becoming a school dropout.

I was soon going to get over distressing and anxious thoughts from looming uncertainty because Bill alleviated my dilemma. He indicated his willingness to take responsibility for my fees and waited for Alan to send his money. If not, he would sustain my secondary education until the end of secondary school when I had gotten a qualifying certificate to look for that level job.

After a few days, Bill p romised to investigate me, accomplish his work schedule for the week, finish his work meetings, and get

15

back to me thereafter. He carried out his investigations and talked to the principal of my school, the late Mr. Richard Ngong, popularly known as Asoka. During their conversation, the principal impressed upon Bill burnished my pitiful plight in life. He reported I was a good student who was needy and in need of help. He asked Bill on my behalf if he could help with my fees while we waited to hear from Alan. Bill compassionately agreed to take responsibility and paid in my fees to form two.

Instead of jumping in ecstasy, I shed tears of joy to applaud God's goodness. The condition attached to the decision was that, as soon as Alan sent a money order to my attention, Bill would get his money back. Alan hadn't sent my fees, and Bill promised to take full responsibility of my fees until I wrote the GCE Ordinary Level. He believed, instead of going into high school, I could write a public service exam for either the police school or teacher's grade one or two program.

Bill did not receive any money from Alan, and the bar proprietor declined to take full responsibility. His own support was to buy books and school needs because I worked at the bar after school. He preferred I resume my bartender job, a plan I strongly abhorred. I didn't want to humiliate myself by becoming a school dropout, and I didn't know how to prevent myself from becoming one. I didn't know how to avoid the insane, greedy request from my boss to resume my bartender job.

If Bill had not show compassion, I wouldn't be writing my story now. God positioned Bill as a favorable and sustainable stepping-stone to suppoty my educational life. "Surely God is my help; the Lord is the one who sustains me" (Ps. 54:4 NIV).

God's interventions were extraordinary and timely. Their sponsorship was an impetus for hard work in school, and that is why I studied impressively and scored good grades on my exams. The transition back to school really energized my zeal to work hard at my studies and to work holiday jobs as he advised.

Bobe Bill Strassberger Inculcates Sustainable Self-Reliance Skills

Bill cautioned me to be self-reliant in order to support my educational pursuits because of my hardship. He suggested I work a holiday job as a coffee picker at the Kom Area Cooperative Union LTD, where he worked. His recommendation that I look for a holiday job was within the Cameroon cultural context that allowed children to work. Hazardous child labor in the United States is considered child abuse but is culturally accepted in Cameroon because children work in some circumstances to augment family income. Our family's financial situation compelled me to work to support my education.

Bill fatefully injected the spirit of determination and hard work that was inherent in my struggles to move toward achieving my academic goals. Since then, I have wrestled with life's ordeals through and through, with many stop signs on my path. By being determined, I became resilient and bounced back in adversity. Despite the hardship I endured, God came to my aid and made an unworkable situation seen with naked eyes as workable.

I picked coffee as my curtain raiser paid job and made 21.000 CFA francs (40 USD). I presented the money to Bill. He added it up and bought my books at a self-help bookshop in Bamenda, which encouraged him to pay my fees for the next academic year, 1983–1984. He had paid 1982–1983 fees just a few months from his arrival. I was overwhelmed with joy for being able to continue school out of my own initiative.

Bill's sponsorship was a threshold to continued education by God's grace

As luck would have it, Bill's compassion provided a leap in my educational pursuits when he paid my fees, and I continued school to form three. As fate would have it, the aforementioned Kom Bum Development full tuition scholarship was launched. I was qualified to apply as stipulated by qualifications set forth by the scholarship board under the auspices of Bobe C. K. Barth.

My application was granted, and it paid my fees for three years until 1986. Bill took partial care of my needs and registered me for the GCE. When he renewed his Peace Corps contract, I visited him in Bamenda. I lost contact with him when he finally returned to the United States.

I learned from him that life was not a bed of roses, and I worked relentlessly to support my education through to master of education level. By taking me to a used bookshop, he injected frugality in order to benefit a cheaper student life with the same resources, like other well-to-do kids possessed. Bill made me the best version of myself. and boosted my self-esteem. My sense of selfhood and self-esteem reflected my new identity. If Bill had not accepted to sustain my education, my schooling would have been discontinued, making me a school dropout, which I hated. By God's grace, he authentically became part of my childhood transition into adulthood.

Lesson from Scripture: Mark 10:45

"For even the Son of Man did not come to be served, but to serve, and to give his life ransom for others" (Mark 10:45 NIV). I learned from Alan and Bill's benevolence that it is not good to turn your eyes inward but to become a true servant by giving to others. It could be in cash or in kind. Alan and Bill made me a better person through giving and sharing. According to the Bible, they are true servants of God.

"Do nothing out of selfish ambition or vain conceit. Rather, in humility value others above yourselves, not looking to your own interests but each of you to the interests of the others" (Phil. 2:3–4 NIV). After learning lessons from Alan and Bill, I am oriented toward giving to others more than taking. They did what the Bible prescribes. I have learned from them to give and share.

Bobe C. K. Barth Fateful In-Kind Support in Secondary School Snowballed to High School Education (1980)

I lost contact with Alan and later Bill and relied

Self-reliance engendered the zeal for continued job searches.

The need to maintain my student status in secondary school as my most cherished goal in life engendered ingenuity. I had to be proactive to overcome my financial pitfalls that had plagued my student life in the early 80s. My peace Corps benefactor Bobe Bill Strassberger had inculcated self-reliant skills as a motivation to support my educational and personal needs while he shouldered school fees and nothing more. These fateful self-reliant skills were the hugest impetus I accrued in my early childhood. Through him, self-reliance propelled me to higher education I enjoy today.

As Peace Corps volunteer, he worked at Kom Area Cooperative Union LTD. He coaxed me to work as coffee picker in the aforementioned union. The Union marketed coffee products for farmers in my village Njinikom. This was my curtain raiser job that spurred the enthusiasm to continue.

Diabolic Sacrificial cultic experience Foiled By God's Grace.

The money I got from the job urged the need to indulge in other holiday job exploits. I had to travel the Littoral Region of Cameroon where my older sisters lived. It was a daring and foolhardy move adventuring out of my village as an unaccompanied minor to chase a second Holiday Job. It was a must go or dropped out of school situation.

My bold decision to travel to the Littoral Region finally procured a job in a pineapple field owned by Mr. Wambo. It was an unbearable and arduous toil but rewarding. The tasks were daunting but I endured the back-breaking tasks and prevailed in attaining my goals. By the end of summer holidays, I succeeded to raise the income for book fees, clothing, and pocket allowance I'd aspired for . I became an upbeat and independent spender. This boosted my self-esteem and selfhood. Mr. Bill Strassberger waited for holiday job income and I had to showcase my worth in meeting my expectations. I needed to be a clean student, with enough books to study and money for clothing and to socialize without pestering him for financial support.

Dweller with a Cultic Associate

The quest for financial solace was doomed by cultic practices in which one of my in-laws, my sister's husband's brother, the late Joe Bangsi. He almost used me as a sacrificial lamb to a religious and devilish cultic association with headquarters in Loum, Cameroon, where they lived. I can't say for sure when he got initiated into that society but I know that he was a bonafied member. The cult in Loum, Cameroon, was mainly made up of wealthy French-speaking Cameroonians. This religious cult of wealthy people was linked to human sacrifices. The cult originated in Nigeria, West Africa. He aspired to become one of the wealthiest elites in my tribe through blood sacrifices. This bloodthirsty cult could be likened to the Illuminati in the United States. The Illuminati are known to have sacrificed many celebrities as a human solstice sacrifice. For those of you wondering why entertainers die at an early age, there may be a reason for that. The Illuminati reportedly have those people killed as part of a ritual sacrifice. They sacrifice to Satan because that is who they worship.

Joe Bangsi yearned to famous and wealthy but his ambitions were impeded by his level of education that ended at elementary level. I was Joe Bangsi's bedmate when I visited my older sister's house in Loum, where Joe Bangsi was dweller. He had nursed plans to build huge glass houses in my village and buy multiple commercial vehicles to start a transportation business. He was a needy man, like me, and suffered under the distressing blows of adversity and hardship. No one knew his intended source of his startup capital for his ambitious endeavors.

Sacrificial event foiled by divine Providence

To complete his devilish mission according to his cultic laws, he needed to sacrifice seven humans to achieve a wealthy and affluent status. Being a member of this bloodthirsty cult, he needed to abide by the laws as an ongoing commitment. These cults of wealthy people in Loum were responsible for the spiraling acts of child and human sacrifice in Cameroon, acts abhorred and condemned by the general public. Human sacrifices were made with diabolic intentions to get rich fast. If the members of the devil cults' sidestepped away from their sacrificial commitments, their wealth would disappear. The punishment for violating the rules and the laws were death, extreme poverty, and insanity and or death by accident or a lightning strike on culprit. My in-law was soon to experience instant insanity.

One night close to end of summer holidays, he lured me into the cult meeting place (the private room) at the Monte Coupe Bar (Mount Kupe) in Loum, noted for cultic practices, and I sheepishly followed him, without a clue what it was. The meeting place was camouflaged to a bar but hosted cultic practices. When I approached the private-room door, some fateful ominous sentiments hit me, and I stepped backward. He came to the bar area and told me to come with him, and I hesitated. All the bar guests were cult members, and the private room, according to reports, hosted the inner core of cultic leaders who initiated members into authenticity. I would have been a victim of circumstance, and you wouldn't be reading my words now.

Divine Providence manifested

Late Joe Bangsi had agreed with the cultic leaders to do a human blood sacrifice of seven humans, with me included. He could only do this in the village because most of his family members had died, and he had no kids to offer as sacrifice for riches and wealth.

He masterminded a plan in my village Tinifoinbi to rally sacrificial victims into a party room. He'd arranged with his cultic boss to appear in a supernatural spirit at 7:00 p.m. to lure victims he had earmarked back at the cult headquarters in Loum. When he arrived at the village that day, he invited a cross section of my villagers to the ritualistic zone to party with him. To him, he threw a casual party because he'd been very ill and recovered. He was penniless but collected items and food from my neighbor, his cousin's (Sam kiiti) store. He hoped that the first deposit of his sacrificial gain would be delivered somewhere in his dwelling place. This would happen upon presentation of his 7 sacrificed humans. As food, he took chocolate powder, pudding, sardines, bread and soft drinks from our closest neighborhood stores. He got soft drinks and candy for the kids.

The party venue was his cousin's house. He'd gone to a neighboring local market to sell his merchandise. The plan was that while at the party, the cult leaders would arrive in a supernatural spirit form at 7:00 p.m. to identify their victims and take their blood. They would later die in some way, according to cultic designs. It could be heart attack, stroke, and or just an accident. No body would know he had been recruited into a blood thirsty cult.

He went out to his cousin's nearby store and bought seven candles to be lit, representing seven intended victims from his cousin's other store house. The cult leaders promised to bring the first deposit of the money he had planned to amass. That would guarantee riches

21

overnight. His cousin had authorized him to use the room for some days before he returned to Loum.

As fate would have it, the other intended victims and I were providentially lucky and protected by the Almighty. Sam Kiiti, his cousin, closed his stall at the Fundong market and made his way home on his bike with his unsold stuff tied to the backseat. When he saw a multitude around his store house, he climbed down from his bike and asked what was amiss. I explained Bangsi's original intention about celebrating wellness after his intense malaria. He said that Joe Bangsi's mom had been ill and almost died and nobody threw a party. Enraged, he stopped the party and dispersed all attendees. On his way to his house he met Bangsi walking back with his seven candles. He told this cultic associate that he had stopped the party. He told Bangsi that there was no reason for partying that evening when his parents were needy and needed money. Instead of giving money to his parents, he wasted on a senseless party and celebration. Joe Bangsi became infuriated and engaged him in a fight. He placed Sam Kiiti in a chokehold and one passersby came to his rescue. Sam Kiiti was liberated from the fight and went home to his house. Unfortunately for Joe Bangsi, it was five minutes after 7.00 pm and he was not back with the requisite candles for the ritual. Most attendees had left, and the door was locked. The perpetrator hadn't access to the party room to execute his intended plan. Out of frustration and realizing the repercussions for violating cultic laws, he had to look for ways to break into the sacrifice room

Insanity watched Live

He into my mom's kitchen and pulled out a machete. He dug out blocks from the walls and stretched his hand to displace the inner door bolt. He succeeded in opening the door, and when he finally got in, he used the machete to shatter all the bottles and the musical set we used for the occasion and started singing. He broke open a pillow and put it like a hat on his head. I watched a scene of instant lunacy.

He had broken cultic laws and punishment exacted was instant and chronic insanity for misrepresenting its interests. It was during his insanity that he divulged his plans to on viewers and attendees of the party. They watched him and said what he'd intended doing with his money got him into trouble.

His parents understood his intentions and knew that there was something wrong. His family members were alarmed when he faked a dance, like the most dreaded juju in Kom palace, the Nkoh. They sought help from a renowned man with psychogenic powers. He explained the intensity of the lunacy and told his parents that if they did not disconnect him from his cultic associations traditionally and through prayers, he would die. He felt ill and developed an unusually big size. His family took him to a renowned witch doctor in Kom, in my tribe, as prescribed by the psychic. The first psychic, Bobe Tim, had Bob Marley–type hair. Joe Bangsi grabbed the psychic's hair, and he told his parents to take him away to some medicine man who tamed violent lunatics. He was finally disconnected from his cultic associations but died a year later, maybe from the results of his cult associations. There was no money, and his life had gone. The quest for fast money may lead us into regrettable endeavors. So, watch out. Nobody ever lured me into any dubious activity after the lessons I learned from this experience.

If God wasn't there for me, I'd been gone by now. Thank you, Lord.

Chapter 3

Fortuitous Prompts Hint a Stepping-Stone to a Catholic Education Job

A lot of reflection and meditation about getting a established job to stabilize my life resulted in fateful prompts for a brighter career. Propitious triggers urged me toward a casual school fees collector and civics teacher job at Providence Secondary School, Fundong Boyo Division. This job fed my zeal after two years (1988–1990) to doctor my résumé by defrauding myself. I modeled it to typify history teaching experience in the eyes of secondary school history teacher recruiters, which was out of the ordinary.

This school fee collector job in which I camouflaged my résumé to represent history teaching experience was a means to an end. I needed work, and it wasn't forthcoming. My attempts to get a good teaching job within the Catholic education agencies of the Archdiocese of Bamenda and the Diocese of Kumbo were fruitless. Inadequate teaching experience might have caused this persistent failure.

Out of frustration, I looked for any menial job, and Providence Secondary School Fundong was my last resort. The school was run clandestinely, and I embraced its furtive values because I planned to misrepresent my civics teaching experience to affirm experience teaching history within a secondary school work environment.

The proprietor was reluctant to encourage me to apply for a teaching job because there were no teaching vacancies, but he indicated there was an alternative plan for me. He made me part of a task force to spearhead the collection of protracted school fees debts as well as current ones. It was a menial job as an advanced-level certificated teacher, but it was a means to an end.

Civics was considered part of the history curriculum within the history department at Providence Secondary School. I planned to doctor my résumé to uphold the experience amassed from teaching civics as proof of experience teaching history. I did this successfully and earned a faked two-year experience that worked favorably to my advantage. I intentionally misrepresented my experience because I had enough subject matter in history accumulated from the GCE Ordinary and Advanced Levels from secondary and high school lessons. I was confident I would be able to defend myself in case any authority challenged my teaching integrity.

I needed a good teaching job to accumulate enough money because I anticipated pursuing further education. I'd tried to teach in lay private schools and mission schools through the Catholic education agencies of Buea and Bamenda, but I was sent packing for being a rookie. I strove to move forward and planned to renew my strength and courage in pursuance for a teaching job within the Northwestern Catholic Education Agency of Cameroon.

The school fee collector job was a gut-wrenching endeavor that unnerved me by the day. I wrestled with my inner self on my inability to achieve my goals. I was unable to support myself with a suitable job but still hoped for the best. I believed in fate, recalling that God had made impossible moves look viable. He'd brought Peace Corps volunteers into my life, all strangers in the beginning who eventually became my sponsors.

I knew that, with God, everything was possible, and I always thought that my life would change for the better. I became ingenious in adversity and hardship. I believed the lifestyle at the school made me an extortionist out of desperation, and the situation pushed me to look for an alternative job within the Catholic Education Agency. Through divine providence, I was employed to teach history at St. Paul's Nkwen Bamenda.

Destiny Conducts Me to a Good Catholic Education Agency Job (1990–1997)

The misrepresentation in my updated résumé to depict the teaching of civics as some history teaching experience was a ploy to seduce employers who needed to recruit authentic history teachers. The purported history teaching experience yielded fruit because the misrepresentation on my résumé reinforced my zeal to apply for a teaching job at St. Paul's Nkwen. My doctored résumé was fake to me and authentic to others who didn't know the game I played with it. I scammed my principal with a doctored résumé out of self-confidence in history subject matter. I became a transformative history teacher and scored good results, reinforcing the principal's decision to renew my teaching contracts.

A providential opportunity occurred during the summer holidays of 1990. I brand this occurrence as divine providence because it intervened to steer me forward unexpectedly when I needed it. I yearned to become a teacher within the Catholic Education Agency and was sent away packing multiple times. Engulfed by feelings of despondence, I didn't give up on my struggles for a better job opportunity, and prayed fervently for the best. I finally got a heaven-sent, and highly anticipated and requisite job offer.

When I visited the late Sebastian Talla, my brother-in-law married to one of the Muenyi's in Ndop in the summer of 1989–1990, I was a beneficiary of God's goodness toward us. During that holiday, I attended morning mass with my host family at the main Catholic church in Bamunka-Ndop.

One morning after mass, I watched Reverend Father Joseph Mbiydzenyuy Ngah struggling to lift a canopy into his car. The church had rented the canopy to celebrate the church's feast day and anniversary. As a parish priest, he had to satisfy all the outstation Catholic congregants.

One morning, we went to a church between Ndop and Banso at a place called Wasih. During mass, entertaining episodes occurred in the church because a bunch of parishioners who suffered from insanity treatable by a nearby traditional medicine man acted humorously, though sympathetically out of the ordinary. During the offertory, one demented patient stretched his hands to take communion, and the reverend father declined.

Another one was singing in a loud voice while the church was quiet. One protested when they turned him away from the queue to take communion because he wasn't a Catholic and not ready for it. On his way back to his seat, he danced very euphorically and wildly without music and seemed amused and elated with himself. The church laughed modestly and not sarcastically because the guy was suffering. I had believed that comedian-type gestures of insanity weren't fun. I later encountered confusion and did the same too.

God is kind to those who follow his ways and believe in him. I am testifying because you are reading from a one-time intense mental health patient who knocked the doors of insanity and death but was resurrected to testify God's goodness. To me, God said, "It is not your time. Yell to the world that good is God all the time."

Golden Help from a Reverend Father, Per God's Design

The bishop of the Archdiocese of Bamenda appointed Reverend Father Joseph Mbiydzenyuy, whom I coaxed for a job within the Catholic Education Agency, to become principal of St. Paul's Secondary School. He fatefully incorporated me into his teaching staff. He was a very close family friend of the Muenyi family, who were very influential church committee members of the Bamunka Catholic Mission and were part of the decision-making body on all church matters. This is how I was connected to Reverend Father Joseph. The reverend father and all other church members were very happy that I helped voluntarily.

I took advantage of every opportunity to network in search of a job. I was optimistic about life and hoped for the best. I had discernibly realized the interworking of God through reverberating coincidences that alerted me of God's presence in my life and hoped for a better life, knowing that, with God, everything was possible. When I learned that the Holy Spirit dwells in us and monitors us by the day, I could easily understand why, during our first religious lessons in primary school, our teachers taught us that God is everywhere and he loved and supported us all the time.

Godly Coincidence

My relationship with Reverend Father Joe Mbiyzenyuy had increased by leaps and bounds. He invited me for dinner, and when eating, he asked about my advanced level grades and the schools in which I wanted to teach. I mentioned Sacred Heart College Mankon and St. Bede's High School Ashing Kom. He indicated that, with two years of teaching experience, he could make a teaching job recommendation on my behalf. Although my résumé had been doctored and updated to reflect the status of an authentic history teacher, I barricaded myself with subject matter learned during my secondary and high school history lessons in case any authority challenged my worth as history teacher.

It wasn't too long after I spoke with him, a propelling coincidence ensued. The archbishop of the Archdiocese of Bamenda, Bishop Paul Verdzekov, acquired Bopson Comprehensive Secondary School to become St. Paul's College. Providentially, the archbishop invited Reverend Father Joe Mbiydzenyuy and named him principal of St. Paul's Bilingual Comprehensive College.

He reported for duty beginning the academic year 1990–1991. Instead of expending energy making contacts to find a place for me to teach in one of the mission schools, he encouraged me to apply to teach European history in his new school. His appointment as principal renewed my hope and courage to become a mission teacher that would propel me into independence and a different lifestyle.

To me, the St. Paul's job was an authentic springboard into a teaching career and other jobs that might come my way. Any human can see the inner workings of God in my life. Propelling happenstances came into play as I moved forward. Fate made an uphill task in getting a Catholic mission job look very easy. Thank you, Jesus.

"Look at the birds: they do not plant seeds, gather a harvest and put it in barns; yet your Father in heaven takes care of them! Aren't your worth much more than birds?" (Matt. 6:26 CEV). Is there such a thing as a coincidence? The way you answer that question will affect the way you give thanks to God. If the blessing you receive is just an accident, you can be glad. But can you be grateful?

If you understand that any blessing comes from God, you can be grateful to him as well as the people he sends to bless you. Our ability to see God's hand in the blessings we receive deepens our faith because we not only see him active in our circumstances. We also see him providing for our needs.

Imagine something happening exactly when needed without any foreplan and creates a positive impact in your life. This is why I felt the need to testify the goodness of God.

Excruciating Scam Dooms Training and Changes Focus on Growth Process

I was a victim of a torturous scam that fortunately altered my destiny in which a confidence man outplayed and deceptively took my money when I was a teacher at St. Paul's Bilingual Comprehensive Secondary School in Bamenda. He intelligibly tricked us when he presented himself incognito and misused the status of his former reverend principal to pry into the anxiety of needy Cameroonians who longed to study in the United States, like me. Once a public relations officer at the presidency of the Republic of Cameroon, he was fired but retained his diplomatic passport that camouflaged his intentions as he advertised stamped visas on mission trips to the United Kingdom and the United States.

The reverend father had nursed hopes to help two good teachers within the Catholic Education Agency to pursue further education in the United States, whom he thought could excel in any academic imperatives of their choice. Unfortunately, he sought help unknowingly from a man he mistook for a modest man, without cognizance to the fact that he was a scammer. The swindler intimated that he wanted two intelligent teachers from Kom (our tribe) to work for the United Nations Development project (UNDP). He pried on my insensitivity to his actions, and I failed to pursue my American dreams. I was fatefully incapacitated to undertake any self-sponsored project because an obligatory teacher training program was impending, and failure to pursue the training detoured the focus of my educational goal to a higher level than the low grade one certification program.

God was in control of my life because he dwells in us and knows us better that we know ourselves. If I pursued the program to become grade one, I would remain a traditional Catholic mission teacher that most people despise, though it is considered a noble job transforming kids' lives morally and academically.

When I talked to my principal about the monetary request and declared my intention to seek authorization as guarantor for a loan from the school cashier in pursuance of the UNDP program, he hesitated and intimated that he was dubious about the program, especially when the issue of money was mentioned in our discussion. He rightfully suspected that the guy who pretended to help me was a defrauder. As I was carried away by vaulting ambition to travel to the United States, nobody could dissuade my ambition to progress by travelling to study and work for the United Nations. I felt a burning need to leave Cameroon and not attend Teacher Training College (TTC) Tatum to qualify as grade one teacher, a lower teacher echelon that I despised without any alternative.

My principal told me that he didn't want to wound my emotions or damage his relationship with me. He reluctantly signed an authorization instructing the cashier to establish a loan of 300.000 francs. I obtained the loan and by God's grace, didn't travel.

The money designated for a specified program to travel was luckily never used appropriately for the intended purpose, and that diverted my destiny. In the beginning I thought his action was misfortune but soon realized that God brought the cozener to light to act as a deterrent to my progress and development to move me forward in a different light toward achieving my higher education goal at the University of Buea that I never dreamed of.

Teacher Training Program Flawed to My Advantage by a Fateful Coincidence

All advanced-level teachers of the Archdiocese of Bamenda were compelled to save and attend the teacher grade one course at the TTC Tatum or lose their Catholic education teacher status. It was a self-sponsored endeavor, and all trained teachers were to become permanent grade one teachers within the Catholic Education Agency for life after training. By God's grace, I didn't attend the program. Obstacles that looked torturous psychologically came to light as propelling Providential interventions.

The applauded results I produced in history at the GCE according to subject classification. A parameter used in grading teacher performance in public exams placed me first twice and motivated the principal to select me to be recommended by the Catholic education secretary for training in the aforementioned institution. It was a self-funded endeavor, and I needed to use my savings for training, as our principal advised. I had nothing saved because the aforementioned distress scam had pushed me into a frugal lifestyle and incapacitated my financial ability to pursue the impending training program.

Even with a thrifty lifestyle, I was unable to save enough to support my education. I equally tried unsuccessfully to obtain support from family members. I looked for ways to preempt a stressful situation, and I approached the principal of St. Paul's to find out if he could violate the new law by giving me another teaching opening, even on casual pay.

He fatefully stated very clearly that he wouldn't argue with the education secretary over the issue and advised me to meet him to explain my ordeal. When I met the secretary, he told me that my recommendation still stood unchallenged and I needed to be trained as grade one or lose my Catholic mission teacher status. I was a little distraught but still hopeful because my hope was ingrained in patience, determination, and resilience. I still hoped for better for worse, but worse providentially made me happier, as you will see God's work in action directing my destiny appropriately.

I contacted family members whom I relied on for help, and they declined to take responsibility. Classes had begun, and my principal indicated, if I weren't ready, the opportunity would be passed over to the next best alternative on the waiting list. Emmanuel, my coworker on the waiting list, accepted and took my place. He secured a sponsor and prepared to go. Emmanuel left Bamenda for Nkambe, his hometown, to get ready but overstayed in Nkambe without declaring if he were ready or not.

Providential Occurrence

When Emmanuel outstayed the registration period, all Catholic Education Agency officials thought he gave up on himself to not pursue the course, which wasn't the case. Father Joseph, my principal, sent me to investigate the status of his registration, and I happily left for Tatum to verify whether he'd registered or not. When I reported to the school, he hadn't registered, and I was delighted that I would authenticate the requisite and uplift my teaching status. I was obliged to get trained, though I hesitated to embark on a lower echelon training.

I called the principal of St. Paul's Comprehensive Secondary School to explain that Emmanuel hadn't registered. He told me to go back to Bamenda to prepare for school. While in Bamenda, my aunt, Mrs. Senocia Tubuo, and her husband sympathized with the situation and offered to help. They coughed up some money, and in addition they got a loan through a family meeting to sustain my training. It was agreed upon, once I completed the program, I would reimburse them. She provided the necessary money 185.000 CFA francs (370 USD) for my personal needs and my fees.

Fateful Day

When I bought all my school supplies in readiness for classes, I went back to Tatum to indicate to the director of the training facility that I had reported, fully ready to enroll. He was making an announcement in one of the classes when the security guy on duty escorted me to the class. When I approached the door, I saw Emmanuel sitting in for evening studies. He had reported to school and registered for classes, and he was seen doing his homework. I was in a state of shock and disbelief about the double coincidence.

The language was very clear here, but I was little disappointed with myself. I stopped short of understanding that disappointments to me had been fateful blessings. Even though the principal of the TTC Tatum was standing near me, I embraced the shock from the coincidence with a smile.

While I waited for a resolution from the principal of TTC, I knew that only one student teacher was recommended from St. Paul, and Emmanuel got it because my intention was frozen by lack of funds. To appease my hopes, I elusively built the determination and energy to move forward, hoping that God would subdue my tribulations and steer my destiny appropriately. The interaction between my inner self and my conscience waved off feelings of desperation with hopes of a better studious adventure in higher education milieu. I actually hoped against hope but prayed that God should renew my strength and courage while I rested in his presence. God guided my intentions and journey to a higher education institution.

I was soon studying at the University of Buea, Cameroon, other than the belittling grade one program. It is discernibly clear how another situation in which something negative happened providentially became a positive manifest here. God is great all the time, and humans should not give up on themselves if there is an objective they want to achieve because, to me, God is good all the time.

I built my life on resilience unknowingly until I read this from a civil rights activist, Martin Luther King Jr., "If you can't fly then run, if you can't run then walk, if you can't walk then crawl, but whatever you do you have to keep moving forward."

God's Goodness Revealed

I was hesitant to commit myself to become a lower echelon teacher when there are hardly any openings for progress. As I kept wrestling with my inner self on decisions and indecisions on my plight as a teacher, I didn't want to resign to torturous feelings by the refusal to not indulge in the training in case I encountered a mishap. This fateful mishap changed my focus toward higher education. The principal of TTC Tatum tried to strike a compromise to not implicate one person unknowingly. The principal of St. Paul's Nkwen had notified him that only one recommended teacher was admissible that year from St. Paul's Nkwen.

I finally made up my mind to seek admission into institutions of higher learning like Ecole Normale Supereur (ENS) Bamibili as a private candidate for the department of curriculum studies and teaching at the History University of Buea, Cameroon. This was an elusive decision out of frustration just to appease my mind because there was no authentic sponsor or guardian. My decision to pursue higher education without any funds in place was a psychological boost to transform grumpiness into happiness because despondent feelings had engulfed me. I had made fateful strides in life and triumphed, and other risky decisions were built on God's love for me, as feelings of hope and achievement emboldened my actions. There were no jobs in my region, and life was becoming exceedingly distressful due to uncertainty about my predicaments. A windfall opportunity had occurred, and I regained my Catholic mission teacher job.

A Lucky Opportunity That Regained My Mission Teacher Status (1994)

When I failed to attend TTC Tatum in 1992, I lived in the St. Paul's Bilingual Comprehensive Secondary School campus and customarily waited for fate to open a job opportunity. The Catholic education secretary proposed to authorize an extra year to prepare me for a higher teacher training professional program. He advised me to seek admission either into ENS Bambili as a private candidate or apply to the history department of curriculum studies and teaching (CST) at University of Buea, Cameroon.

I applied to ENS and providentially got slapped up in favor of application to an institution of higher learning. His proposal to pursue higher education instead of a grade one teacher program thrilled me, and this met my original intention. I didn't know how to overcome the tribulations inherent in my livelihood to afford higher education, but I relied on hope and fate.

Fate and destiny had sorted out very murky situations to provide directional clarity of purpose. If I attended ENS Bambili as a private candidate, I would have become a permanent Catholic teacher without hopes of continuing university studies because the diploma issued upon graduation still needed qualifying courses for a degree. Fate and destiny blocked private training for a diploma and detoured me to a bachelor's degree program.

My hesitation to not quit my dwelling place from the St. Paul's Nkwen campus without a job opening earned a fateful gift. Some students sought admission to repeat the GCE in St. Paul's Secondary School at St. Paul's. The school became a high school and created an overload of both first- and second-cycle work. Most teachers taught both cycles, and shuffling between junior and high school burdened the teaching staff of the exam classes. The heavy workload created temporary openings, requiring a casual teaching assistant in the junior school.

The providential occurrence was by the authorization of the high school section by the bishop of the Archdiocese of Bamenda, which changed the status of the school from a secondary to a high school. St Paul's Bilingual Comprehensive Secondary School became St. Paul

Comprehensive High School. If the inception of the high school were not authorized, I wouldn't receive the luck I got.

The principal assigned me to take over some of those openings in the junior school. I supported the arts department in subjects like English literature, economics, commerce, and history. I was assigned principally to take care of the reseated students in European history. They paid me between 5.000 CFA francs (2.50 USD) and 10.000 CFA francs (5 USD) a month. It was somewhat an on-call, casual position without any contract. I was paid the aforementioned amounts out of the benevolence of the principal of the school, who had requested that a special account be kept for all repeat cases. I used the money for taxis to look for jobs. Even in this situation, I still sent support money to my younger brother in school in Government Secondary School Fundong.

The Opportunity from Casual to Part Time: The Beginning of the Journey to the University of Buea: Fateful Opportunity on a Sad Note

A fateful opportunity occurred when one of the arts teachers, Mr. Asongwe, died and created an opening during the 1993–1994 academic year. As fate would have it, the school needed a teacher to sustain the academic life of the kids. The principal offered the position to me, and I accepted it on a part-time basis. The school cashier was to pay me 40 CFA francs (80 USD) per month. I earned 80 CFA francs for the last two months of the academic year, and I was ready to impress the school administration in order to regain my most-needed teaching job.

Before the year ended, the Catholic education secretary promised a one-year contract. I needed to save and prepare for school. My target institution was not TTC Tatum to become grade one. Now the coincidence that blocked my ability and zeal to a grade one course turned my attention to an institution of higher learning, and my choice was the University of Buea.

New Syllabus Fortuitously Opens Threshold into the University of Buea, Cameroon

The Cameroon GCE Examination Board had developed a new history syllabus to replace European history, my main teaching subject at St. Paul's High School in Bamenda. The new history curriculum covered European history and then merged it with world, Cameroon, and African history. The new curriculum sidelined me; I could only teach parts of the subject. So I couldn't be a full-time teacher. I needed to further my history education to become a full-time high school teacher.

I didn't know how to achieve my higher education dream without a sponsor. A supernatural force sorted out my pathway to growth because only God knows what happens ahead of humans. God influenced the creation of an Anglo-Saxon university, and I was qualified to apply. The undergraduate helped my continuous education exploits.

Fate at Work

When I wrote the GCE Examination Advanced Level in 1988, I passed but didn't attend the University of Yaoundé, because of financial constraints and the university offering a disqualifying and frustrating series in the arts department derived from the French system of education. This university policy fatefully distorted and slowed my academic progress. In that series, an unintentional bias impeded history student attendees to select their needed courses toward achieving their dream academic goals. My intention was to study history in that university, but history couldn't be studied as a single subject. Instead, it was merged as history and geography (or histoire/geo in French) combined.

If I had to study at the University of Yaoundé, I would go for English, but I declined applying into the English department because many English students had graduated and remained unemployed. The supply of English teachers surpassed the demand. I was compelled to look for a job, and the only hope at that time was teaching. I looked for a teaching job, and that led me into the University of Buea in 1997, nine years after graduating from high school.

As luck would have it, a presidential decree transformed the University of Buea from the school of translators and interpreters into a full-fledged Anglo-Saxon university. In this regard, I was able to apply into the department of curriculum and teaching of history. If the University of Buea were never transformed, I wouldn't have attended higher education. Just by divine intervention, I was able to attend the prestigious Anglo-Saxon university, Buea in Cameroon, when all other mishaps steered my destiny toward that university. Though I had very little saved, I took the risk worth taking, and by the grace of God, I graduated with an undergraduate degree in curriculum studies and teaching of history in 2000.

The excitement of going to the university was exhilarating. It was good to be a university student nine years after graduation from high school. It was a long wait, full of positive and negative activities. I welcomed the positive happenings and endured those that were seemingly challenging and unachievable. I had hopes that life would be different with new accomplishments.

The sum total of my savings amassed from palm wine sales and the little left over from my St. Paul's pay was just about 100.000 CFA francs (200 USD). I needed books, tuition, and fees. Out of my money, half was set aside for school fees and other imperatives. So I held the other half in reserve.

After my failed attempts by God's will to not attend TTC Tatum, the Catholic education secretary recommended I apply to the department of curriculum studies and teaching of history, at the University of Buea, Cameroon, to gain a professional degree in teaching history. I was admitted in June 1997, and classes started in October. It was a period full of anxiety because I had been out of school since 1988 and had not taken any education courses. My main overthink was not the anxiety about studies, but how I would take care of lodging and food.

As earlier stated, I had no direct sponsor and had to rely on people's benevolence, as was always the case in the past. I felt guilty that God had helped me too much and might quit when I needed him most, but the good Lord came to my aid in a timely fashion. I told myself that God does not give up on people he loves, especially those who live by his will.

The Catholic education secretary had urged me to embark on a secondary or higher education program to authenticate my degree and teaching status within the Catholic Education Agency or lose it. I investigated living conditions in Buea and learned that student life was expensive. The news about the expensive life in Buea frightened me amid indecision to undertake university studies without a sponsor and no savings. In my preparatory research to assess the living conditions there, I learned that one of the most charitable Kom notables, the late Mr. David Teh from my village, provided free lodging to needy students in a wooden rental mini cite in Buea.

He was the most generous man from my tribe that God had positioned as a fateful stepping-stone toward my academic and livelihood imperatives. If he hadn't provided free lodging, I wouldn't have continued going school and wouldn't be writing my memoir from the United States. God is great all the time.

Timely and Precious Room Offered by a Selfless Human

I hadn't connected with David to notify him before I departed to Buea. Approaching him to get help was key to the assistance I needed. I had heard that he seemed unapproachable from his tone, but he softened as soon as he established a cordial relationship with shorthanded humans in dire need of help, like myself. My younger brother, Raphael Tasah, worked in Douala and was a sole proprietor of a small store. I hoped, if all else failed and I was desperate, he would come to my aid. He agreed to be my backup support as needed, though without taking full responsibility.

The agreement motivated me to leave for Buea. I packed up my stuff and boarded a Jeannot Express bound for Buea. My destination was unknown, and I feared the unexpected. I suspected that bad luck might befall me and I would carry shame reloading all of my stuff back to my province.

I arrived in Buea in the evening. I didn't tell anybody I was going, so nobody expected me, even though I knew a few friends from my village who lived at the Chia Jua Mini Cite, where I hoped to be a dweller. I relied on some friends for direction, those who were equally needy dwellers on how to settle into student life in Buea. Emmanuel was my main contact. He advised me to visit David's Buea town residence to report formally and make any request for lodging. David was the only person to authorize needy dwellers from Kom to live in his mini cite.

When I reached his residence, I knocked at the door. He acknowledged my presence and asked who knocked. I acknowledged my presence and announced my name. He asked what I came for, and I made it clear that I had all my stuff from Bamenda and left my luggage outside his Sosoliso mini cite. I didn't want to explain my reason for going to him but explained my situation to tell him why I was in dire need of help. I indicated that some relatives mentioned him when I investigated embarking on a professional education program at the University of Buea, Cameroon.

I pointed out that helpless friends had declared his selflessness in giving out free rooms to needy students and I had come to ask for one. He specified there was always a big rush for rooms and it was necessary to preannounce my intention before I left for Buea. He asked if I knew anybody whom he knew and could relate me to. I told him I had two prominent aunts, namely Mrs. Senocia Tubuo and Mrs. Hortensia Njuakom. He immediately recognized the names and softened his tone.

I was not frightened and became more explicit. I told him my school and work history. He chastised me for arriving unconventionally without any notice. I feared, if he got mad at me for my unexpected arrival, he could reject my request for a room, which would disrupt my zeal to study. I went on my knees and begged him to help just one more desperate person. I explained, and weeping, I offered up pathetic sentiments to make him feel pity for me.

I pointed out that I came to Buea University by the recommendation of the Catholic education secretary. I further cajoled him by impressing that, after graduation, I would resume work in one of the Catholic high schools or secondary schools in Bamenda.

He mentioned, if I were pursuing a professional program, he would want me to take any empty room, but he feared that all rooms might be full. Divinely speaking, there was a gracious one to be allocated to me. In my upbringing, I upheld the attributes of determination and resilience, not giving up and bouncing back in adversity with hopes to move forward. Despite many stop signs on my path as I progressed in life, I achieved successful and self-applauded moments by the grace of God.

The allotment of a self-governed room took off a financial burden on rent and stabilized my focus on my book work. The room alleviated expenses of needy students like me who were incapable of affording rent and university tuition. This benevolent gesture scored the privilege to study at a prestigious Anglo-Saxon university. This incentivized other kids and me living under the same conditions to work hard in school.

In trying to put in more effort and determination, I won two university academic scholarships. I was able to graduate like other well-off kids because God had made impossible situations in my life look viable without a sponsor and backup income.

The bachelor of education degree in curriculum studies and teaching of history from University of Buea, Cameroon, impacted my application to the master of education degree program at the University of Minnesota. Without a free room, I wouldn't be reporting my story. I led life on a string by God's grace and thrived. I illusively misjudged Gods mercy with the believe that my sufferings will miraculously disappear in favor of God's blessings for a better life.

This independent dwelling place lifted the financial burden from my shoulders in the face of adversity and hardship, and that smoothened my pathway toward achieving my educational goals. I had a sum total of my savings accumulated from palm wine sales and on-call teaching at St. Paul Comprehensive Secondary School in Nkwen Bamenda. When the scammer tricked me and took my money, I started a palm wine bar to save for school.

I had no direct sponsor, and I had to rely on people's benevolence, as was the case in the past. I felt guilty that God had helped me too much and might quit when I needed him most. I told myself that the good Lord does not give up on people whom he loves, especially those who live by his will.

As aforementioned, I was compelled to be trained or lose my lucrative mission teacher status. Just after two semesters to complete the first year of the three requisite years to complete my undergraduate program in curriculum studies and teaching of history, I ran out of funds and envisioned becoming a school dropout during the third and last academic year. I hesitated but envisioned life ahead of me rooted in distress. In that predicament, I talked to my well-off relatives and friends, and nobody offered to help.

Felicitous Parliamentarian of My District Sustains My University Education

Worrisome thoughts stressed me. Plagued by exhaustive thinking, I had a propitious prompt overnight that urged me to talk to Honorable Paulinus Jua, a parliamentarian of my district, Njinikom Kom. On a Friday at midnight, I got an optimistic hint to visit his residence to solicit help in favor of my back-to-school fees.

I walked to his house very early in the morning and rang the bell, and he opened the door. He hadn't seen me for a long time and asked why I visited him unexpectedly early without notifying him. I stated explicitly that I needed fees for my second year to accomplish my course registration. I indicated I would love to get a total of a 50.000 CFA francs (100 USD) to achieve my ultimate goal of completing my training program in curriculum and instruction at the University of Buea, Cameroon. I impressed upon him, if I didn't have school fees, I would stop my education, which would have a ripple effect on a highly valued teaching opportunity. I equally hammered home the fact that I went to the University of Buea on the recommendation of the Catholic Education Agency of the Archdiocese of Bamenda to be trained to teach history.

He declared he didn't have money to pay my fees at the university but proposed raising a loan if I agreed upon his proposed amount repayable after graduation. There was a flicker of hope as I prayed silently to God to push luck onto me. If I didn't have school fees to register for my third semester, which was supposedly the beginning of my second year, I wouldn't continue school.

Fortunately, God urged him to make up his mind to help. He didn't have direct cash but sent me to his laundry services manager to give my year's fee for the 1998–1999 academic year. His manager paid 30.000 CFA francs (60 USD) and later 20.000 CFA francs to make up 50.000 CFA francs (100 USD). I was able to register for classes because my compassionate older sister Christina Tasah and brother Raphael Tasah, all living in the economic capital of Cameroon, promised to help logistically with food and pocket allowance.

An Unprecedented Request for Marriage as a Fiancée's Dad Fatefully Dooms Relationship (1998)

In 1991 I fell in love with a girl, Kimberly. I dated her for two years, and she became my fiancée in 1993, as she was a better choice for a wife then. I visited her parents' house on many occasions to seek authorization to take her out to a seafood dinners and nightclubs.

According to our agreement, marriage was promised upon completion of my training program recommended by the Catholic education secretary. In 1994, her dad urged me to sign a marriage contract to take my future wife out of his house. I rejected an unprecedented and unconventional request for marriage against the will of both fiancé and fiancée. His action was ominous, and I ran away packing. Not too much later, I heard she had had fiancé number two. In this case, I had to look for a different woman friend because I'd envisioned total futuristic animus from Kimberly's parents in the future, which could hook her into the loop if we got married.

If she had finally gotten married to me, she might have abandoned me during my traumatic illness, especially when my wife had to take me to medical facilities, clean urine and emesis, and pull me around. God has given us well-behaved and smart kids in school, and I do not believe that the blend of the biological composition derived from Pam and I wouldn't come from Kimberly. I thank God for seeing ahead of me and taking care appropriately.

Lucky Move Helps during the Last Year of University Studies (1998)

When Honorable Paulinus Jua helped me to avert the ordeals of a school dropout, I was still determined to complete my undergraduate degree without any source of revenue to accomplish my last year at the University of Buea and qualify for graduation. Muddled by uncertainty on my inability to continue school, I begged God for mercy. My prayers resonated with the Holy Spirit, and I got the help I needed for one more step forward.

During the summer holidays going into my third year, the marking of the GCE Ordinary and Advanced Level was advertised to take place in Buea and Bamenda that pertained to the Anglo-Saxon tradition instead of Yaoundé when the Ministry of National Education ran the GCE. The creation of the Cameroon GCE Board was fateful because I wouldn't have had a holiday job that was made easy by my residency in Buea as a student.

Now that the Cameroon GCE Board conducted the marking of the GCE in Buea and Bamenda, secretariat workers were a requisite resource for markers to accomplish their duties. I knew nobody within the organization, but I was in dire need of a holiday job to raise school fees and a sustainable allowance in order to be upbeat when school resumed. As fate would have it, I got propitious conscience prompts to visit the GCE board selection committee of the GCE secretariat workers.

An urgent prompt that I strongly believe was the work of the Holy Spirit signaled a move to write a pathetic note about my predicament getting back to school because of lack of funds. I did it as conceived and shoved the lucky note under the door where GCE board members met. Just by God's mercy and love, my name was called to participate at the GCE secretariat. I worked impressively to the end of marking session and raised 70 CFA francs (140 francs). I paid 50.000 CFA francs for my fees and saved some for books. If I didn't get fateful prompts to write a note to beg for help and if there were no compassionate official to identify with my plight, I wouldn't work and would agonizingly drop out of school. I thank God for everything.

Chapter 4

A Teaching Job Disappointment Becomes a Blessing Per Divine Providence (2000)

"And we know that in all things God works for the good of those who love him, who have been called according to his purpose" (Rom. 8:28.) When I discerned God's goodness in my life, I recalled fateful, propelling, and transformative coincidences navigated my destiny. Since then, I cast myself at Jesus's feet so he might renew my strength and courage while I rested in his presence to move me forward. Every disappointment is a blessing to every born-again child of God. It's a strong belief that God sometimes works out his plans for us through tribulations like in my case. So we need to face all our life challenges with a kingdom mind-set or perspective. Until a born-again child of God understands that God doesn't allow problems in his or her life to break but to make him or her, he or she will always live a frustrated life. I haven't led a frustrated life because my livelihood is imbued in hope and positive blessings rewarded major disappointments.

During my childhood transition into adulthood, I encountered feelings of sadness from multiple displeasing setbacks, but I didn't give up my struggles. I haven't allowed disappointment to subdue my passion of becoming well off. Instead I turn to God for mercy, and my life has changed and is changing. God is good all the time. Be fervent in your prayers to trigger miracles in your life.

> Disappointment is delayed appointment. Disappointment will strengthen but will never destroy. When disappointment travels towards you, you must be determined to meet it with courage. Never give in to disappointment, hopelessness or despair. When you overcome disappointment, you acquire the strength to change your disappointment and turn it into an appointment. Nobody can avoid pain. Pain is inevitable and pain comes through disappointment but you can do something about your situation and be determined to walk through the darkness of disappointment into

the light of your appointment, your destination. An African proverb says, "Smooth seas do not make skillful sailors". You cannot run away from trouble; trouble will always come. You cannot avoid pain, it is inevitable. The difficulties of life are intended to make us better. A path with no obstacles leads nowhere.

I am my own man today because of my relentless and courageous moves I took in adversity and hardship. I went to the University of Buea under the recommendation of the Catholic education secretary, the main employer of the Archdiocese of Bamenda, to pursue a professional teaching certificate at the University of Buea. Per the education secretary's contract, I was compelled to regain my teaching job in any Catholic mission secondary or high school upon graduation.

When I graduated in August 2000, I duly reported to the Catholic education secretary to present my results. He was thrilled by my performance and requested I report to his office on the Catholic mission teacher recruitment day to regain my Catholic Education Agency job. He finally recruited and sent me to Sacred Heart High School Mankon Bamenda to meet the principal and authenticate my reemployment. I would have been the most qualified teacher on his staff with a professional degree earned from a new program created in the mid-1990s by the Cameroon GCE Board, which was compatible with the new syllabus for the current year.

I was soon to encounter a merciless principal, a reverent man who became repulsive per God's design and fatefully became a large detour that influenced my future. I follow God's grace in my journey toward success in life. Situations that looked cumbersome and unalterable became uplifting.

"We deserve nothing from God. God does not owe us anything. Anything good that we experience is a result of the grace of God" (Eph. 2:5 KJV). Grace is simply defined as unmerited favor. God favors or gives us good things that we do not deserve and could never earn. "Rescued from judgment by God's mercy, grace is anything and everything we receive beyond that mercy" (Rom. 3:24 NIV). Common grace refers to the sovereign grace that God bestows on all of humankind, regardless of their spiritual standing before Him. Saving grace is that special dispensation of grace whereby God's sovereignly bestows unmerited divine assistance upon his elect for their regeneration and sanctification.

Obtrusive but Fateful Bulwark Getting My Most Needed Job (2000)

When I returned from the University of Buea as a professional undergraduate teacher, I reported to the Catholic education secretary, the main teacher recruiter for the Archdiocese of Bamenda. When I handed over my employment letter to the reverend principal, his awkward demeanor astounded me when he read the appointment letter. To me, it looked as if I wronged someone unknowingly, but I recalled that I came to get my job description and extracurricular assignments.

He put on a grim and disdainful look and intimated that I wasn't qualified to teach in his school. He was a fateful bulwark on my journey to my most desirable, which impeded my ability to not become a high school teacher. That impediment directed my focus toward higher education. So I modified my intention to not teach in a lower echelon, but incidentally I focused on pursuing higher education at the University of Buea, Cameroon, for a master of education degree program in educational leadership at the University of Buea, Cameroon.

Luckily there were no openings, and the university authorities advised me to report back at the beginning of the first semester of the next academic year. Had there been an opening to register for the master's degree program, I would have taken the risk to continue school without a sponsor. Divine intervention intercepted my ambition to study because enrollment had been suspended. Destiny conducted me to meet the Catholic education secretary of the Diocese of Buea. Reverend George Nkuo of the Diocese of Buea, now bishop of the Diocese of Kumbo, told me to look for an alternative teaching job as the ultimate source of solace.

I was astoundingly sent packing from Sacred Heart High School Mankon for being a rookie teacher. Being the new guy isn't always easy. I wasn't a beginner in the teaching field because I had amassed a plethora of history teaching experience from 1990 to 1997 at St. Paul's. The professional program in education was a move to nourish my subject matter and teaching skills in order to be competitive in the job market, but I encountered a mind-boggling rebuff that brushed me off.

I visited Reverend Father George Nkuo to take advantage of any available job opportunity. He made multiple calls all around the Diocese of Buea and got feedback that all subjects had been distributed and the teaching timetables were full to capacity. When he reported that there weren't any openings in his agency, I knew I would be unemployed and once again doomed to loneliness and idleness. Just by divine intermediation, the principal of St. Francis High School, Reverend Father Joe Awoh, announced that he needed reinforcement.

The education secretary, in agreement with the principal, sent me to the school for unspecified duties to acclimatize with the work environment. I reported for duty, and the principal authorized me to work as assistant discipline master. In executing my assigned tasks, a fateful attack by student thugs commanded by Anderson finally earned a useable bank statement and subsequently a visa.

If you establish the connections imbued in God's interworking that make you a better person, you will ascertain the role of divine providence.

Fateful Decision to Block Culprit's Dismissal Wins a Bank Statement and Visa

A recalcitrant student named Anderson donated in-kind support to my pursuit of a visa to study in the department of human resources at the University of Minnesota. Anderson's father was a very wealthy businessman, and he finally gave me a bank statement.

Anderson was infatuated with two female friends in his class. From investigation, there was no practical intimacy. He thought that buying food and sharing money with the girls made them his. He developed a deep lust for the female friends whom he fantasized about.

In between there was an identity issue. Each claimed ownership out of pride. There had been mounting animus toward each other that triggered clashes in an airborne dwelling in which one of the girl's face was scratched and the other was bitten on her right shoulder, leading to excessive bleeding.

We had an emergency discipline council meeting to figure out how to curb and/or resolve conflict among adolescent peers. We invited Anderson's parents to school to form a transformative parent-teacher effort to figure out how to transform Anderson, but the young man thought his dad was the larger problem.

Anderson was the epicenter of conflict in his class over money and love. The main cause of these disciplinary problems emanated from abundant pocket allowance from his cocoa merchant father. The funds became a distraction to his studies. He squandered it on numerous adventures with his peers. He couldn't concentrate, which engendered a sharp decline in his academic performance.

My attacker scaled the fence to eat outside the school as well as watch erotic video shows around the school neighborhood. He despised the refectory food and termed it dirty because he thought the food was improperly cooked.

The flow of cash enticed an attraction to Anderson by girls in his class and beyond, especially some senior students alike who wanted a share of his money. He became a star, though his stardom was short-lived by his father's curtailment of his student allowance in school. The move subdued Anderson's excitement, and he became focused on his studies.

I took a fortuitous decision to block his dismissal without any clues to his father's wealth. My leniency to preempt his punitive discharge from school was the working of destiny in my life. The school officials consented to my proposal to not dismiss him from school. Instead my disciplinary cohorts branded the culprit as a delinquent burden on me and didn't envision a change in his waywardness. They thought I was myopic and my blind confidence in him was misplaced trust. They pointed out that a second attack on me was imminent. They sarcastically stated, when I fell along my journey to appease the suspect, they would give me the help Jesus got with his cross on his journey to crucifixion. "A certain man from Cyrene, Simon, the father of Alexander and Rufus, was passing by on his way in from the country, and they forced him to carry the cross" (Mark 15:21 NIV).

I conceived and masterminded a plan to transform Anderson's unyielding and uncooperative attitude. His main disciplinary concerns were entertaining girls, loafing, and scaling the fence to buy basic imperatives he preferred. His recurring scaling of the school fence engendered wayward behavior that brought him to grips with the discipline department. I chose to subdue his recalcitrance by issuing permission slips to visit their home when in need, and I invited his father to visit the school upon request. Anderson was better able to stay within school boundaries and genuinely exited the school fence on permission.

When Anderson's father reported to school, I explained his disciplinary ordeals. I pointed out that his son had become a dissipated loafer who wandered around the school during evening studies just to say hello to his girlfriends and couldn't concentrate on his studies. I impressed to his father that, to help his son, he needed to reduce his pocket allowance, which spurred his motion to scale the fence out of school and engage in other deviant behaviors.

Anderson's father was upset with him, so he took my advice and reduced his allowance. I lousily told him that Anderson had two girlfriends in his class who hovered around him exploitatively all the time. His student life would be continually disrupted if his activities remained unchecked.

His father gave him a mild reproach and intimated that Anderson would be withdrawn from school if he clung to his delinquent tendencies. Anderson got mad at me, and we bypassed each other multiple times without greeting. I reported his attitude to his father, and he encouraged me to be as diplomatic as possible because his older brother had resigned to juvenile delinquency and abandoned school prematurely. There was a likelihood he might follow suit if we persisted squeezing Anderson to change. Anderson's father suggested I make him my friend because, if he felt uncomfortable and isolated, he might bolt from school.

One fateful night close to lights-out time, an all-city power failure occurred and caused a total blackout. The students got excited and acted otherwise. This excitement caused an uproar that ignited into indecent behavior among the students. A cross-section of students exhibited disorderly conduct. In acute darkness, students became rowdy, played on their desks like they were drums, and made unbearable noises. I couldn't contain it because I was the only discipline master in school during evening studies.

Most of the teachers scheduled to supervise evening classes that evening had abandoned their duties. In that uproar, I instructed all the students to return to their dormitories. Students made illegal and pleasurable visits to opposite-sex dormitories. Younger students ran up to me and reported that students stood in dark corners and kissed. This was against school rules and were serious crimes.

The whole environment was chaotic. I escorted the girls to their dormitory, and on my way back to my office to write up an incident report in the school journal, thugs with rocks attacked me. That night a shower of medium-sized rocks fell on the chapel roof, where students and the St. Francis community went for church services on Sundays and weekly morning masses. They decided to attack from a holy ground when I was cutting through the sports complex by the chapel as I headed to my office.

I intended to write an incident report on the chaos, which erupted that evening when a rock landed in the middle of the sports complex and missed my left ear. Another one missed my shinbone, and three others were shot simultaneously and continuously from different directions.

I covered my face and head with my hands because I didn't know which part of my body to protect first. I cried out aloud for help when the principal's cook, Gabriel, approached from the residential area. He asked what was amiss, and I reported that delinquents had attacked me. He had a very strong torchlight and flashed it on the main plotter of the attack, Anderson.

After my investigation, I discovered he was angry because I ridiculed him to his father, and the resultant effect was a sharp reduction in his pocket allowance, which impeded his ability to spend freely on himself and his girlfriends. This became a huge disciplinary issue.

The principal, the senior discipline master, and I had a brief meeting and figured out what to with the case. The senior discipline master was in favor of instantaneous dismissal, and some of us decided that we should invite his parents to address how we would handle the situation.

At the time I took this decision to block his punitive discharge from school, I didn't know about his father's personality and wealth. It was the working of fate to take an impactful decision from my knowledge of adolescent psychology amassed from my professional training program in curriculum and instruction at the University of Buea, Cameroon. I fatefully cautioned them that, in teenage years, kids develop adventurous propensities. His choice to throw rocks at me might have been excitement to attack the discipline master in revenge and make fun of it with his peers in the dormitory or at school.

His father was invited again. He was sure his child would be dismissed. Just by divine intervention, I told Anderson's father that I would handle the case and make his son my friend.

We convened another meeting with the principal, the duty week masters, Anderson's class master, and the senior prefects for a final decision on him. Almost all attendees at the meeting advocated dismissal, but I objected to such a lousy decision. I advised the discipline council of the school that it didn't make sense devaluing children's growth process with frequent dismissals. I pointed out that my knowledge of adolescent psychology intimates that children be groomed and counselled but not discharged punitively from school.

All my actions fatefully worked to my advantage. I promised to subdue Anderson by showing concern and love to subdue truancy in order to remodel his behavioral situation and finally make him my very good friend. I signed his permission slips to forestall his frequent scaling of the fence to get the items he preferred to get. I got food for him from the refectory and modified it in my house to taste homelike. He always visited to eat and then became very gentle and loving. He performed well in his exam into form four.

My visa search was still underway, and I'd been sent away packing four times. Destiny pushed into a qualifying bank statement that gained a visa. That same year, my admission letter was still pending while my visa application was continually denied because of no authentic proof of sponsorship. Optimistic prompts visited my conscience, which to me was God speaking directly to me.

So I conceived the idea to ask for a bank statement from Anderson's wealthy cocoa dealer father. I felt empowered to ask for a bank statement because I'd helped his son from a wayward truant into a subdued, modest, and well-behaved kid and I needed help from him in return. I just thought of an adage in elementary school in Cameroon. It says, "One good turn deserves another." I expected favors from him in return of my transformative gesture on his son. God rewarded my move.

My fourth appointment was August 13, 2003, and the visa officer gave me the bird for the same stigmatizing reason noted by the first visa officer during my gut-wrenching interview, "not qualified to study in the United States." After a few days, the director of foreign affairs sent an invitation email to my attention to report to the consulate.

At this juncture, I was elated by the invitation from an embassy official that ignited into a flicker of hope now that a top US Embassy official was involved in my case. I didn't envision what was at stake, but I hoped for divine intervention alluding from previous instances in my life that were unmanageably cumbersome. And God came to my aid. I had become distraught by the multiple dismissals I'd endured in my previous interviews. As chance would have it, I had an official invitation from an embassy official to report back to the embassy to meet him regarding all my visa credentials.

The foreign relations officer, Thomas Santacana, had asked key consulate workers why I continually visited the US Consulate with the same passport and the visa officers didn't take me seriously. The string attached to the invitation to the US Consulate in Yaoundé, Cameroon, was to come with my sponsor, Anderson's dad. This was ominous because I feared he would turn down my request to report to the US Consulate to defend my visa because he was a big cocoa dealer and my request was at the peak of his cocoa business in Cameroon at that time. No conscientious businessman of his caliber would risk his profits to defend the interest of somebody he met casually through his child. He hesitated steadfastly for a week or so, and I didn't relent in praying for divine mercy from my Jesus.

Excepts

"Eternal Father, I offer you the body and blood, soul and divinity of your dearly beloved Son, our Lord, Jesus Christ, in atonement for our sins and those of the whole world. For the sake of His sorrowful passion, have mercy on my visa process and on the whole world."

The intervention of God in my visa pursuance was remarkable and commendable. As a Catholic Christian, I pray the Chaplet of Divine Mercy incessantly on a daily basis at three in the afternoon. I have experienced positive changes in my life, and I guess it is God's grace and mercy. Even though I was fraught with frequent dismissals for not being qualified to study in the United States, I had trust in God that my visa pursuit would be fruitful. I had gone a long way paying visa fees at every step of the way. I assembled myself and stayed firmly true to the fact that bad luck sometimes makes me stronger and determined while I continued praying for mercy. I was confident that I had a genuine sponsor and a qualifying intellect to study. This made me assertive to persist in my quest for a visa as long as I envisioned a glimmer of hope on the horizon.

Divine Providence Manipulates My Sponsor to US Consulate to Defend Visa (2003)

My sponsor authorized an affidavit of support and a bank statement to confirm his ability to sponsor my education in the United States. These documents consolidated my armor toward my visa search and created flickers of hope on the horizon. A huge impediment I envisioned was to convince my sponsor to report to the US Consulate in Yaoundé, Cameroon, and authenticate my affidavit of support and the bank statement he gave me to present to the visa officer as needed. He was hesitant to leave his business to visit Yaoundé at my behest because of the nature of his business and the amount of money he would lose at the peak of the cocoa season.

At the time I called him, he was at the Douala seaport to send his cocoa shipment to Europe and the United States. I had an old phone from my wife because I had never gotten one for obvious reasons. I used it to communicate with Anderson's dad. I invested time on prayers, begging Holy Mary, mother of Jesus; Jesus; and the Holy Spirit to intercede. By the will of God, Anderson's fatefully changed his mind and reported to the US Consulate in Yaoundé. God had helped, for only he has the power to influence challenging situations to move me forward.

Anderson's father's decision to change his mind to visit the consulate on my behalf was fateful. I'd luckily transformed his son from a wayward boy into a cultured, well-groomed, and decent person. He knew my political affiliations and helped me to leave Cameroon. What would happen if his son didn't attack me viciously with rocks? I wouldn't know him and wouldn't get the help I got. What would happen if I endorsed his son's dismissal from his truancy and vengeance? I wouldn't get the requisite bank statement for my visa and wouldn't be educated. I wouldn't be in the United States, and I would be lost in my village.

If someone doesn't believe that God exists, I am sure my story may help attest my assertion to the realistic belief that he does and performs stuff that goes unnoticed and unannounced. There are several gifts from God that humans never pay attention to and/or testify about until we face danger. When atheists who do not believe that God exists confront a life-threatening and/or dangerous situations, most victims exclaim, "O God!" This shows that most humans acknowledge the existence and love of God and his help mostly in times of need.

The visa officer on duty interviewed my sponsor separately from me. During the interview, there was a providential happenstance in which the visa officer asked my sponsor if he were married and had children. He answered yes on all the questions, and I was lightened. The visa officer tickled him that, if he had children, my university tuition and fees would be a huge burden, especially kids' school and feeding.

Fate came into play here, especially when the officer asked how many children he had, and he said three. I had told my previous officer that he had three kids, and the officer noted this on my file. I didn't know the composition of his family and forgot to ask him in advance to be consistent because, if I misspoke and contradicted him, the officer would feel I lied. And that might have hampered my visa issuance.

The officer issued my visa after the somewhat traumatic interaction with my sponsor, which made me believe that God endorsed my visa search and acquisition. The visa officer opened my file and pulled out all the refusal slips for all four visits. He reversed the one on my fourth visit and wrote, "Visa granted." My visa was made available after a protracted fight.

I went outside the consulate and kissed the tar mark with my tongue. I looked up to the sky, as if I would see God. Both hands were raised, and my palms were open as if to receive a gift from an official.

I said, "Thank you, Jesus! I believe in your personal love for one so sinful and worthless as I am. Heart of Jesus, I put my trust in you. You have made me a better me."

Chapter 5

Heaven-Sent Project Supervisor Awards a Visa and Reconnects My Peace Corps Friends

D r. Christine Swanson served as a Cameroon Peace Corps volunteer at the University of Buea, Cameroon. She was my instructor and end-of-course project supervisor at the aforementioned university in the year 2000 when I rounded off my studies. Five students were placed under Christine's supervision, and I was one of her team cohorts. I profoundly thought that fate positioned her as my project supervisor for a reason. In this way, I told myself that I was lucky with the Peace Corps. I would use Christine to solicit help toward pursuing my educational goals in the United States when she returned to her homeland.

When she left, I took her email address and wrote to her after a year. She worked at the International Student and Scholar Services (ISSS) at the College of Liberal Arts at the University of Minnesota. I asked her to help with my application process into the University of Minnesota, and she accepted. Additionally she accepted to pay my application fees with her credit card to accomplish all registration formalities when I was still in Cameroon.

I was brainwashed by a stereotype that all Americans were rich, so I asked my academic advisor, Lori Cohen, who worked in my department, for money. She dismissed the idea just as I mentioned it to her. Christine had lived in Cameroon and discerned the truth in my desperation. God knew why he placed me under her, as you will see.

When I got admission to the renowned University of Minnesota, she supported my visa process, especially when I was disdainfully dismissed multiple times for not being qualified to study in the United States. She talked to the coordinator of the human resource development program, Professor Gary McClean, and the director of ISSS, Dr. Thomas Kay. They both wrote to the US Consulate to remind them that I was academically and financially upbeat toward my studies. On my fifth visa appointment, I got it. Here are the excerpts of interactions between Christine and the director of ISSS in her effortful endeavors to me.

The Director of the ISSS, along with Dr. Christine Swanson, Contributed to My Visa Process

Christine wrote,

> Dr. Thomas Kay was the director of International Student and Scholar Services (ISSS) at the University of Minnesota. I remember you connected really well with her. It was the other Kay (Kay Orner) who picked you up at the airport. As ISSS director, Kay Thomas was concerned about you getting a student visa. She called people and sent letters. I e-mailed some Peace Corps people and finally connected with the public relations officer at the US Consulate in Yaoundé. The visa was approved (late), but Kay Thomas told me to tell you to come right away before any other complications could come up. You arrived a couple of weeks after the semester had started and had to work very hard to catch up on your classes. But you did it! Kay Thomas, Kay Orner, and I were all impressed.

Christine exhibited African hospitality more than Africans do. Fate blew me away from relatives and friends from whom I could solicit lodging needs in a strange country by God's design for an important reason. Before I left Cameroon, I had been told that life was expensive, and I missed investigating to know why. I was insensitive to the plight of international students without any clues of financial hardship inherent in studying in the United States. My relatives and friends declined to take responsibility for my lodging and other needs and left me in limbo. I was at the mercy of Christine, who epitomized hope and continuity by her hospitability.

When I got the visa, I learned that student life was expensive in the United States. I encountered heart tremors because of uncertainty about my plight as an international student in the United States without any authentic sponsor. I feared stigmatizing myself by becoming a school dropout out of desperation. A multitude of detractors was waiting to laugh and denigrate a poor child attempting to revitalize and balance his status with the associates of the lucky wealthy ones. God had donated opportunities that helped me to move up my academic ladder. I relied on destiny to conduct me appropriately, drawing from past experience in which light shone on darkness and opened my way forward. No Cameroonian offered to help with my lodging needs at all.

Luckily Christine was gracious enough and arranged lodging in her neighbor's condo. God blinded the minds of all my well-known friends and family friends by influencing them to reject my request for lodging in their homes for a reason. I soon realized that Christine was God's stepping-stone to a better life, like all well-to-do students in the United States, upon my arrival. By living with her, she created history by doing what she did to me.

When the eighty-five dollars I brought from Cameroon ran low, Christine discovered I was stressed because of the fears and difficulties I embraced upon my arrival to the United States. I couldn't buy basic stuff and starved at school. She questioned what happened to the money my sponsor declared at the US Consulate, and I stayed mum to myself for private reasons.

My intention to apply for asylum to live under US protection was impending, and I didn't want to look like a liar if I told her. She mentioned in one of our dinner conversations that Cameroonians go to the US Consulate and trick officers to get visas. And when they report to the United States, they encounter insurmountable difficulties. She said, if I were unable to eat and take care of myself, she would report my current situation at that time to immigration officers.

I sensed that my life in the United States was grinding to a halt because my situation was tantamount to homelessness or deportation. I feared deportation because reentering Cameroon would subject me back to my troubled life that I wholeheartedly dreaded and abhorred. I would be humiliated and demeaned by detractors who despised my progressive strides and longed to watch the poverty of the neediest child go protracted from bad to worse.

According to some, no human ingrained in poverty like me should see the light that leads to life, but Jesus was my supportive pillar. He showed me the light and led to life. I was never going to witness darkness. "Jesus spoke to the people once more and said, 'I am the light of the world. If you follow me, you won't have to walk in darkness, because you will have the light that leads to life'" (John 8:12 NIV)

How I Got the Light that Leads to Life

When I was agonizingly distraught with looming fears of the unknown, I stood in the middle of nowhere while hopes on all fronts were dashed. I fled from Christine's arranged condo and took refuge in the room of a friend, Ngwainbi Emmanuel, on Ruth Street in St. Paul. He was in transit to Canada with a departure date two weeks from the day I packed my luggage to his attention.

He said to me, "My brother, I am a Canadian resident. I will be here for two weeks and resume my station. Where will you live while I am gone?"

My head spun in imagination, wondering what would befall me next in my grievous tribulations. I felt rejected by my friends and relatives. I envisioned homelessness, and with only forty dollars from the eighty-five dollars that I took along with me to the United States, I was helpless but hopeful. Christine knew I was downcast and had no phone. She sent an email requesting I report back to her neighbor's condo, my lodging place under her supervision, as quickly as I could in order to adjust my lodging and feeding needs before I departed formally. I was afraid to return because I didn't know what would happen next. I felt I had betrayed her confidence on me by not reporting my asylum story but still stayed mum.

I hesitated and prepared to disappear into the Cameroonian community in Minnesota, but no one helped. My heart tremors intensified, and I dreaded deportation. But a call from God appeased me, "Go back and get help."

I resigned to fate in God and felt compelled to return. I felt, if she pushed me harder a little more about my financial situation, I would speak my truth as the last resort. I planned to divulge that the bank statement was just a way to get me out of Cameroon because my sponsor felt pity on my political troubles in my country and didn't want a good man, as he branded me, to be deported to Cameroon. In this regard, I would tell her why I planned to file for asylum.

As fate would have it, I asked how to reconnect to returned Peace Corps volunteers who helped me in Cameroon and were back in the United States. She gave me a catalog of updated emails and phone numbers of all returned Peace Corps volunteers, and I was able to reconnect with Alan and Bill two decades after which I lost contact with them.

Alan took over responsibility for my rents and needs that stabilized my livelihood, and Bill advised me on American culture and what it took to mar or make a fortune in the United States. Through Bill's advice, I didn't get involved in criminal activities and maintained a good moral rectitude record that earned my asylum, permanent residency, and US citizenship.

If God weren't there for me, I wouldn't have made it. If Christine didn't accept to receive me at the airport, I wouldn't have any address to identify my lodging place with and would face the aforementioned ordeals of hunger, homelessness, and/or deportation. If a Cameroonian relative or friend chose to satisfy my lodging needs, I couldn't go to Christine and wouldn't be able to reconnect to my most-needed Peace Corps friends of Cameroon. I feel that God positioned Christine as a pivotal connection stepping-stone to reconnect my Peace Corps friends of the early eighties with me. God manifested his presence and worth when Alan and Bill reentered my life when I was in dire need of support in their country. Luckily they were well off and compassionate, as before in the early eighties. Thank you, Jesus.

My Peace Corps Benefactors of the Early Eighties Luckily Reenter My Life (2003)

When I fled from Christine's supervised dwelling place and reported back to the negotiated condo, divine providential intervention manifested and revitalized me to feel proud that God had his eyes fixated on me for his goodness. I asked her how to reconnect with returned Peace Corps friends of Cameroon who'd served in Cameroon and were back in the United States. I described my relationship in detail with returned Peace Corps volunteers and invoked Alan's and Bill's benevolence when I was pretty young and desperate.

I recounted that Alan had sponsored my secondary school and Bill took over responsibility when Alan left unexpectedly for the United States. Being at the mercy of our provident God, I was lucky to reconnect with my Peace Corps sponsors of the early eighties. Christine told me that she had a Peace Corps directory of all returned Peace Corps volunteers who'd worked in Cameroon and were back in the United States. The manual contained updated names, emails, and phone numbers of all returned Peace Corps. I looked by first names and didn't find them. I went by last names and found "Lakomski, Alan" first.

I copied his information and looked for "Strassberger, Bill." I got his details and wrote down his contact information as well. I called my friend Terence Komtangi and told him that I'd love to use his phone to make some urgent and important calls. He told me that he worked and could only give me a ride the next Sunday. He picked me up and took me to his apartment, and I used his phone to call. When I got the information on Bill and Alan, I called Bill first. I did not get him and left a message. I called Alan and spoke with his wife, Pam, because he had run an errand in his neighborhood. I gave my name to her, intimating, when Alan came back, he should call me.

Pam asked for a contact phone number, and I gave her my friend's number. Alan called back and asked where I was calling from. I said Minnesota. He asked the reason for my visit to the United States. I indicated that I came to the United States on an F-1 visa for international students to study at the College of Education at the University of Minnesota. He asked who was to pay my fees, and I didn't know how to explain. I was a political activist in Cameroon and planned to live in the United States permanently, but I hadn't talked to any immigration officer and stayed mum. He asked where I lived, and I explained I was a dweller in a temporary condo prearranged by Dr. Christine Swanson, my end-of-course project supervisor in the department of curriculum and instruction at the University of Buea, Cameroon, where I rounded off studies in 2000 in quest for a bachelor of education degree.

He said I'd better give him Christine's number. I did. He talked to her, and she explained my tribulations to him. He asked about my sponsor, and I didn't know how to explain. But I told him that my sponsor gave me a bank statement and confirmed the affidavit of support at the US Consulate in Cameroon. I had an immigration story but hadn't talked to any immigration officer and stayed mum. I explained the bank statement was issued by BICEC Bank Cameroon, and the bank officials promised to remit the money as needed. I had just forty dollars left in my wallet. He said, whatever arrangement I'd made with my intended sponsor in Cameroon, he was compelled to send five hundred dollars to Christine because she was bored with me and hadn't included me in her food budget.

She didn't foresee an extension of my temporary stay of two weeks according to the protocol arranged before I departed from Cameroon to be protracted. Alan sent the money and advised I should read notice boards to check if I could find a roommate and share rent. I did and got one with a Chinese professor, Dr. Youxin Gao, of the human genetics department on the St. Paul campus of the University of Minnesota.

The room was 720 dollars, and we split it, 360 dollars apiece. Alan promised he had a plan to send five hundred dollars a month for my rent and advised I should be frugal and save up more than my rent money to get food. He paid my rent until I graduated in 2005. I attribute the luck I got in this instance to divine intervention. Alan was alive, well-off, and still as compassionate as before when he met me in Cameroon in 1980. He had a good job as a chief operating officer at Global Medical Staffing in Utah. He was able to take care of his mortgage and pay my rents. If he didn't have enough to eat and take care of his home mortgage and me concurrently, I would have missed it all.

What I admired most was Alan's wife, Pam. She was the epitome of compassion, just as compassionate and sympathetic as her husband. She empathized with my situation, which fed her zeal to agree to take money out of her family income to support my livelihood at age thirty-four getting to thirty-five. If they didn't agree on my plight, I guess I would be telling my story from Cameroon. I thank God for setting up a difficult but learnable and rewarding journey toward becoming an authentic adult.

My relatives and friends who gave rides to me and ensured that I should watch homeless people on the streets made me feel I would be the same, but God and all shamed them. Thank you, Jesus.

Godly Lesson Here

I once lost contact with both Alan and Bill and didn't know if and when I would reconnect with them. I reflected about them, wondering if they were alive or dead. Each day I went to the world map and perused through the North American map, I looked for Utah and located Salt Lake City, where Alan lived after he returned from his Peace Corps volunteer service.

Alan played a pivotal role in my life by setting precedence and allowing destiny to take its course. Bill entered my life because Alan jump-started my schooling and I was able to continue my education. I didn't relent in pursuing my academic goals and used my self-reliant skills inculcated by Bill to push my way through to the University of Buea, where I encountered another Peace Corps volunteer, Christine, who reconnected me to them.

I feel that God kept two indispensable humans alive and temporarily away from me in the early eighties. They were strangers to me and eventually became my sponsors. God suspended the help they gave me in Cameroon and saved the requisite assistance for my future unknown to me until I reported to the United States. The help they would have contributed to paying my fees and taking care of my needs in Cameroon was saved so they could come to my aid in the United States when I faced the ordeal of hunger, homelessness, and deportation. One can easily recognize the goodness of God and my inclination to Christianity. "The LORD is good to all; he has compassion on all he has made" (Ps. 145:9 KJV).

I can testify to God's goodness toward me in every situation in my life. You may have followed all what God has done to me. From bartender and manager of a confidential brothel to an American citizen, holding a master of education degree in human resource development from the renowned University of Minnesota, is commendable. I thank God for all.

Chapter 6

Late Arrival to a Class Study Group Fatefully Gives Birth to A Private Loan from a Course Mate

The 2003–2004 academic year started September 2, 2003, the same day I got a hard-fought visa in Cameroon. Upon my late arrival on September 11, 2003, to the United States, student orientation was over, and classes had begun. Unable to proceed with any academic imperatives, the director of ISSS, Dr. Thomas Kay, advised me to report to the academic advisor, Lori Cohen, to help with my registration formalities.

According to the semester requirements, each full-time student was compelled to register for a total of six credits derived from two major courses of three credits each. If an international student of my caliber violated this rule, deportation was imminent. Lori registered me for two courses that remained open for the semester: AdEd 5101, "Strategies for Teaching Adults," and HRD and AdEd 5002, "Survey in Human Resources."

My Strategies for Teaching Adults instructor, Dr. Baying, gave me a hearty welcome and commended me for my patience and resilience toward my educational endeavors. He put forth all course requirements and an accomplishable syllabus through to the end of the semester. He just murmured to himself to my eavesdropping that I did not orchestrate the visa delay. The State Department workers, not me, caused the delay. Gary McLean had informed all teaching and clerical staff that I would be running late because I had sent an email to him about my visa and travel itinerary.

The next move was to meet my instructor for Survey in Human Resources. I met her, just to confront a hard-hearted woman. She stereotypically waved me off by intimating that I wouldn't cope with the course. For fear that I wouldn't register six credits from two courses, I went to the coordinator of the program, Gary McClean, to be sure I registered for two courses. I would have violated the new immigration law, SERVIS. After 9-11, the Department of Homeland Security instituted the aforementioned law, and any international student who violated it faced the loss of his or her student status, and deportation was practically imminent. The SERVIS software reported student activities to the Homeland Security online database.

When I met Gary, I reported my course instructor's condescending attitude. He brought me to her class, just to experience a rebuff.

She dismissed me with the back of her hand. "Go, go, go. You can't cope with this class. This course is a survey of all the courses in the human resources department program, and lateness will only result in a failed grade, an F, for you."

She didn't want me to register for the course when it was still unknown to her that there were two openings available. Perplexed by all these troubles, I reflected on a sermon in a Presbyterian congregation back in Cameroon when a pastor preached on the subject, "God knows why."

By God's grace, I skipped several hurdles in my growth process as I progressed, and today I am my own man. "All things have been committed to me by my Father. No one knows the Son except the Father, and no one knows the Father except the Son and those to whom the Son chooses to reveal him" (Matt. 11:17 NIV).

I envisioned that completing my master of education degree program would be unconquerable, so I invested my time in prayers. When I overstepped insurmountable hurdles and made a headway in life, I appeased myself that, no matter what difficulties I encountered on my way up, it was God's decision to keep me afloat. I prayed silently to myself by the day.

> Behold me, my beloved Jesus. Weighed down under the burden of my trials and sufferings, I cast myself at your feet that you may renew my strength and my courage to move forward while I rest here in your presence. Permit me to lay down my cross in your sacred heart, for only your infinite goodness can sustain me. Only your love can help me bear my cross. Only your powerful hand can lighten its weight. Help me, Lord Jesus, because I put all my trust in you.

By relentlessly praying, God blessed me with an amazing well-off course mate from Korea, Jack Jewoong, who came to my aid with an uplifting loan to complete my fees that had attracted a hold that blocked my second semester registration. If he didn't lend me the loan, I wouldn't register for second semester and would fall out of school. That was tantamount to loss of status that would cause deportation to my home country, Cameroon. I believed in divine providence from the time I earned the trust of a Peace Corps philanthropist, a guest friend at the bar where I worked. He projected my self-esteem and selfhood. Since then I welcome fortunes and misfortunes, believing that God nourishes my plight with benevolent and positive gestures.

Divineness of Negation Portrayed

When my Survey in Human Resources instructor excoriated and threatened to exclude me from her course, I reported the case to Gary. He beckoned on me hurriedly to her class and made it clear to her that I was compelled to register for two courses. She didn't welcome the news with delight. Instead her countenance altered, and she wore a grim look on her face and asked me angrily if I would cope with the course, as I had just come late from Cameroon when student orientation was over and classes had begun.

I was agreeable to carry the load of the course, but her awkward demeanor and attitude exasperated me. She hesitated and pointed to the fact that the class had already been sorted into groups of four team members each. She intimated that all the students had started understanding their team members, and my late arrival would disrupt team cohesion. I told her that I was very qualified for the class and ready to endure impending difficulties that I might encounter. She angrily accepted me into the class and auspiciously placed me as a fifth member of a group that was composed of students from Asia, Canada, Puerto Rico, and Africa (myself). I was soon to be a beneficiary of her timely hesitation to incorporate me into her class and the eventual permission to join a God-sent team.

Divine Providence Manifests

I humbly testify to the glory of God I know and the God that I hope you will gain a glimpse of throughout this book. To show that

God loves me, one of my course mates, Jack Jewoong, became a good friend and gave me a loan from his year's tuition and fees. I registered my courses for the second semester. If Jack did not give me the loan and I did not receive my older sister's support from Cameroon, I would have discontinued school. Jack was entangled by the support I gave him during the first semester and didn't want to study alone. The coincidence placing me in Jack's group, the fact that Jack didn't know enough workable English and needed my assistance, and the knowledge I was not savvy in computers and needed help from Jack was a triple coincidence to get propelling help toward my human resource development degree.

Heaven-Sent South Korean Student Friend Sustained My Student Life (2004)

When the first semester ended, I owed an outstanding bill of forty-five hundred dollars. I was compelled to pay it in full. At the beginning of the second semester, once classes started, a hold was placed on my University of Minnesota online account, which blocked access to my student account and hampered the selection of requisite courses to complete registration for the second semester. There was a pop-up on my student account each time I attempted to sign in that warned that my accumulated debt had to be cleared in full before I registered for my courses. The protracted feelings of becoming a school dropout that had followed me on my academic journey smacked me again. I was helpless and bemused.

To mitigate my registration dilemma, I contacted Alan to assemble all the funds he'd earmarked for my rent for the whole year in order to pay off my outstanding tuition and fee debt. He impressed the fact that forfeiting my rent in favor of my tuition and fees was not a very good idea because there was a likelihood of becoming homeless in the United States. He warned that the experience could be agonizingly traumatizing for an international student. I didn't take offense when Alan turned down the request.

When it was almost certain that I wouldn't continue school, I told my course mate from Korea, Jack Jewoong, that I was very certain to drop out of school. He shook his head in disbelief and mentioned he had money in his account at TCF, the university bank at that time.

He indicated that he could be my loan guarantor if I were interested in taking out a loan. I was unsure about repaying it because I was financially desperate and without any authentic source of income. I was bound to accept the loan offer in due course because I had no alternative on the horizon when I had a high propensity to study.

I accompanied him to the TCF, where both of us were members. His intention was to guarantee a loan of twenty-five hundred dollars for my fees, but there was a backlash because of insufficient funds in my account. The loan manager on duty asked for our bank cards to pull up our accounts, and we provided them. He opened Jack's bank account first. It was heavily loaded with all his fees for the whole year. He opened mine and was startled. My account showed a total of seven dollars. He wore a light smile on his face that quickly changed in a second into a grim look.

He asked why I came to obtain a loan with only seven dollars in my account. I pointed out that I desperately needed to pay my tuition and fees to register my semester courses, but a hold on my account impeded my ability to complete my course registration for the second semester. I told him that I had a promise of a student job at the University of Minnesota bookstore, and that would serve as collateral to repay his money as soon as I started work.

He was a little skeptical, as his looks portrayed. I got a propitious prompt to mention my culture core project I worked on from which I could use to pay his money back. His fears abated, and Jack agreed to be my surety in case I defaulted on the loan. I explained that Jack had offered to make available a loan of twenty-five hundred dollars but was worried about my ability to repay it, considering my desperate financial troubles, which he was aware of.

I told him that Jack wanted to use the bank statement as a backup document as proof in a court of law if I defaulted on the loan. The manager in turn intimated that he had never handled such a premature loan request from a customer of my caliber with a very limited credit history. I did not understand what credit history was all about, as I was just new to the United States. He felt pity for a newcomer to the United States, as he discerned from my looks and my raw accent. He finally explained it was the confidence that customers exhibit to establish proof of their reliability for repaying what they owe. Reliability in some situations depicts honesty that builds trust and confidence in relationships.

He dialed the phone to handle a transaction while I stood up at his desk and listened keenly what he had to say. I mistakably thought he was calling the police because I might have violated the bank's loan policy to borrow money without any collateral security with insufficient funds in my bank account, and I fled. I ran out of the bank in winter and slipped on black ice into a puddle. I fell on my left side and was bruised from my left shoulder to my thighs. My clothes were shabbily drenched in snow and ice water.

Jack called me back and said there was no offense in making a loan request in the United States and I should come back. I refused.

Jack accompanied me to my room and asked why I'd left Cameroon to study without sufficient funds for fees and other survival income. Though I was desperate, I did not want to wash my dirty linen in public, and I kept my financial woes to myself. He carried the impression that I was very poor, and that worked to my advantage. My financial situation was irrevocable, and I accepted my penury as I grew up to meet it.

Out of frustration, I saw myself standing in the middle of nowhere. He felt pity on my situation but was grateful for the support I gave him during the first semester in our teamwork effort that earned good grades for both of us. As luck would have it, he was deficient in English and proficient in computers and vice versa.

Both of us worked interdependently, and I became a huge resource for him likewise. My ability to support him in English in which he was in dire need of help was fateful. He hated studying alone and preferred to be my study mate instead of American students, which was beneficial to me in the end. According to him, he was uncomfortable soliciting help from American classmates because, as a South Korean, he found the American accent difficult to process and preferred to study with me. He wasn't comfortable with the American accent because, to him, it was cumbersome to process the American English into meaningful words and sentences, and that slowed his learning process and made learning cumbersome.

He was very computer savvy and helped me immensely with many computer processes that I used throughout my graduate studies.

I foolhardily encouraged him to authorize the loan release. I assured him that he would regain his money as soon as I started work at the University of Minnesota bookstore. I reiterated that the bookstore manager was very positive about a job opening for me. He based his hopes on my impending job and the Culture Corps project that he witnessed me working on.

Jack agreed to authenticate a transfer of the twenty-five hundred dollars into my account needed to pay my fees and register for classes. My only collateral security for my private loan was my monthly rent support allowance that I got from Alan and the Culture Corps project that he'd witnessed me working on. I had made a proposal and a plan with the coordinator of the Culture Corps project at the ISSS and was paid a thousand dollars.

Jack had more confidence in my project proposal confirmation. He was aware of my intellectual aptitude and knew I could climb mountains with any academic endeavors. His courage and benevolence thrilled me. Even my relatives and close friends could not take the risk he took.

When I told Jack that my Culture Corps project had been approved, he said he wasn't surprised because he knew my academic worth. Being intelligibly assertive was a big contributive factor in my growth process. If God did not give me the intellect and reasonability from commonsense, I would be trapping crabs in my village now. Thank you, Jesus, for uplifting my selfhood and boosting my self-esteem. If my parents were all alive today and heard that the Peace Corps volunteer who visited our homestead to get permission to sponsor my education in 1980 was my friend in the United States, elation would add more years to their life. May God rest their souls.

I worked with Jack in two courses, and he felt he did well on his first semester results because of my contribution to his studies. He believed he would encounter insurmountable difficulties accomplishing his graduate degree without my assistance. He was sure that my Culture Corps project would be approved and paid for. He knew I would repay his money.

I told him that Alan sent five hundred dollars every month, and when I paid my monthly rent, I had a hundred dollars remaining and could squeeze money out of that for him. I indicated that, against all odds, he would receive fifty dollars each month until I was paid for the Culture Corps project. He took the highest unimaginable risk a student could take without any surety to safeguard repayment in case I defaulted.

He finally invited me to TCF and orchestrated a transfer of twenty-five hundred dollars into my account. My older sister, Christina Bi Tasah, had sent 1.000.000 CFA francs (2,000 USD), so I had a total of 4,500 dollars, which completed my fees. He accompanied me to Frazer Hall, where the student financial services offices were located.

When we accomplished the transfer, I had paid my first semester fee, and I was ready to register for second semester courses. I was overwhelmed anew by the joy of becoming a student. I thanked him for the risk he took to initiate the loan.

As a fully registered student, I authenticated my legal status as one of the prerequisites for application. By becoming a resident, my tuition and fees dropped by half. I was qualified to apply for a student loan, which I did, and that helped me to complete my graduate degree in human resource development at the University of Minnesota. Jack was God's donation, and together with my older sister, whom fate enticed to send a million thousand francs that got converted to twenty-five hundred dollars, this facilitated the payment of my fees. This recounts how I meandered my way to a master's degree status.

Heaven-Donated Culture Corps Project Secures Loan from Course Mate

As an international student, I visited the director of ISSS, Dr. Thomas Kay, to ask for financial aid. She had written to the US Consulate when my visa request and application was turned down multiple times. I thought he was part of my struggles and would come to my assistance in times of need. She said financial aid was unavailable for international students because all international students thrived on the declared sponsorship ability for tuition and fees before entry into the United States, as stipulated on form I-20.

I was perplexed because I had nobody to turn to and nowhere to go. In this regard, I turned to God in silent and spoken prayers using this quote, "Call upon me in the day of trouble: I will deliver thee, and thou shalt glorify me" (Ps. 50:15 KJV).

As fortune would have it, the University of Minnesota Senate voted to launch a scholarship program for international students called the Culture Corps project toward the end of the first semester. The Culture Corps was a new program to promote internationalization on the Twin Cities campus of the University of Minnesota. Through Culture Corps, international students provide education and knowledge to the university community, bringing their distinct international perspectives to the classroom and department activities. The goal is for international students to assist faculty and departments in classroom or nonacademic activities. In return, they receive a scholarship award credited to their STARS account during the term of the project. Awards at this level are not considered financial aid or employment.

I worked on the project and fatefully got a scholarship on it paid to my student account. I had gotten close to Dr. Thomas Kay by continually pestering her for financial aid to support my education. He dismissed the idea in many instances, intimating that international students didn't qualify for any financial aid and grants because that legally applied to Minnesota residents, and I wasn't one yet.

My Culture Corps project topic was "Work, Community, and Family: The Case of Cameroon. Meanings of and the Relationship among Work, Community, and Family. Northwest, Adamoua, and Far North Provinces. Examination of Cultural and Historical Contexts and Philosophies."

When I completed the project, my supervisor, Dr. Ruth Thomas, advised, to complete the project, I had to provide education and knowledge to the university community and bring perspectives that pertained to Cameroon to the classroom. She was a professor of family education and invited me to many of her classes to present on patrilineal and matrilineal succession in Kom, Cameroon. I presented classes on the succession question in Kom, my tribe, in which nephews succeed uncles instead of sons succeeding fathers. I also talked about the rural woman, the rural man, and child labor in Africa and Cameroon in particular.

She was impressed by the presentation and stored it in an electronic file in the McGrath Library at the University of Minnesota. Dr. Thomas Kay approved the project and insisted it be put in the university library. The project was put in an electronic version even though other university authorities wrangled over my pay that was to be credited to my university account. Some officials opposed my pay because my immigration status had changed from international student to resident.

I was eventually paid six thousand dollars, credited to my student account. As luck would have it, the money I received over and above my Culture Corps earnings facilitated the repayment of all my private student debts, especially the one God gave me through Jack Jewoong.

I was psychologically balanced and concentrated on my internship project at the University of Minnesota that qualified me for graduation. I remained on legal immigration status and qualified to apply for asylum.

Chapter 7

Political Activism in Cameroon in 1990 Providentially Helps Asylum Process (2004)

WWhen I finally paid my tuition and fees, I refreshed my student status and authentically remained in a legal status. When I accomplished second semester registration, I was qualified to file for asylum in the United States to seek protection against the repressive and autocratic regime in Cameroon. The changes started in Bamenda when an opposition party called the Social Democratic Front (SDF) forced its authorization through protest marches, sit-down strikes, and ghost towns.

This was during the political upheavals that began in 1990, after the launching of the SDF, the main political party in Cameroon. The SDF advocated for the right to free speech, the need for a parliament elected by the people, free and fair elections, and the need for a liberal government elected by the people. I upheld these democratic principles when I became a member of the SDF in 1991. The Catholic Education Agency recruited me in September 1990 to teach history at St. Paul's High School in Nkwen, Bamenda, the epicenter of political turmoil.

The political changes in Cameroon were fateful because I was employed to teach history at St. Paul Bilingual Comprehensive College, Bamenda, which became the epicenter of political activity and fortuitously absorbed me into political activism. I joined the SDF in 1991, and the presidential elections of 1992 were widely believed to have been won by John Fru Ndi, the chairman of SDF, but the victory was hijacked by the ruling government in connivance with the Cameroon Supreme Court. The refusal sparked widespread peaceful political protests, though protesters encountered violence and killings. President Paul Biya declared a state of emergency in the Northwest Region, where Bamenda was the epicenter of activity in 1992. These political events in the early nineties fed my asylum story.

I later joined Southern Cameroon's National Council (SCNC), an offshoot of the SDF that propagated federalism, in 1997. The quest for a federal system spurred the need for a federal system of government that I strongly advocated for, starting in 1997. It spurred further unrest. The fateful orchestration of luck in my life brought to bear some significant events in my life. I never knew revolutionary events in Cameroon in the early nineties would have a ripple effect on my livelihood in the United States where I sought asylum.

I reported torturous experiences I'd encountered in the early 1990s and beyond in Cameroon to the Center for Victims of Torture in Minnesota. When I arrived the United States on an F-I visa, I told one of my mentors that I wanted to remain in the United States because I feared returning to my home country of Cameroon after my university studies.

I asked the procedure for changing my student visa to a resident visa. My mentor said the process was cumbersome and, if I participated in the peaceful political changes in my country, I might have a credible story to file for asylum. I agreed and told him that I was a member of two political organizations, the SDF and SCNC, which were involved in peaceful revolutionary changes in Bamenda, Cameroon, which happened to have been the epicenter of the political upheaval that spread to the whole country of Cameroon.

The Asylum Process (2003–2004)

The Center for Victims of Torture requested a comprehensive personal statement. I reported on my personal statement as requested, and the Center contacted the people, the parties, and the powers I mentioned in my report to confirm its authenticity.

They got back to me, reporting it was credible to file for asylum in the United States. They advised me to report to the Minnesota Advocates for Human Rights because they had immigration lawyers to help me to establish my asylum case for free. I provided the answers to all the questions the Minnesota Advocates for Human Rights requested to be explained in the report.

Minnesota Advocates for Human Rights did their research in the United States and Cameroon and advised me to file for asylum if I had genuine fears of returning to Cameroon after my studies. Minnesota Advocates for Human Rights stated that my personal statement was credible for filing for asylum and living under American protection. They intimated, if I taught history and kept on comparing the political system in Cameroon to the United States and the French revolutions, the Cameroon government would in reality consider me a subversive element. I would be at risk if I lived in a repressive and autocratic regime like the one that prevailed. They said those arrests would never stop. I was encouraged to file, and I tried to make facts available and coherent.

Minnesota Advocates for Human Rights assigned an immigration attorney to guide me in the whole asylum process. It would only work if I were a full-time registered student. The appointed attorney was to choose a University of Minnesota law student intern to work with me. I accepted the offer to work with the law student intern. The designated attorney advised me to continue going to the Center for Victims of Torture for healing and mental modeling that would boost my psychological mind-set in preparation for the asylum interview.

The supervising senior lawyer was Karen Ellington. She and the intern did a pretty good job on my case. Karen accompanied me to my asylum interview. It went pretty well, and she gave me a hug after the session for a job well done. It didn't take long before I received the letter that granted my residency under American protection. I was granted asylum on August 1, 2004. I later became a permanent resident and am now a citizen of the United States.

Permanent Residency Gives Birth to U.S. Citizenship Fully Integrated into United States

When I received asylum and became a permanent resident and subsequently a US citizen, I worked full time at Fairview Southdale Hospital Edina as a parking services specialist. At the job I developed diabetes, and I was discharged unjustly. I was distraught by the belief that I had maintained a good work record and ethics and didn't envision being fired. I was distressed by traumatic feelings that led to depression. I encountered some intense memory problems that were compounded by an immune system disorder and a nervous system breakdown. These illnesses attracted God's miracle in my life.

Chapter 8

Traumatic Illness: Death and Resurrection by God's Grace

When I was wrongfully discharged on June 7, 2013, from my Fairview job, I accosted my boss to inquire why I was callously exuded without any probable cause. She put forth flimsy excuses, intimating I misused my scheduled work time, making frequent nonwork-related trips out of the office for my personal needs. To her, I was supposed to use my break times only. She further explained that the parking department at Fairview Southdale was slim, as its budget needed employees to concentrate on their jobs to raise more revenue to catch up with department expenses. In that regard, I was required to work time on task.

I had been diagnosed with diabetes, which required frequent use of the restroom. It was difficult to hold urine, and I'd disgustingly urinated on myself multiple times. My firing shocked me because I had maintained a good work ethic from 2006 when I got the job until diabetes hit me in late 2012. I started making annoying mistakes and needed medical attention but was sent packing. Stressed, I got lost in thought many times.

Depression kicked in, and exhaustive thinking ignited into confusion. I encountered an immune system disorder that ravaged my white blood cells. My CD4 cell counts were evaluated to just one and made immune system defenseless. By this, I encountered an incomprehensible nervous system breakdown and lost coordination entirely. I unintentionally misspoke. I didn't know myself and my kids, and I was helpless. I needed 24-7 home care, and my illness weighed down on my family, especially my wife, who grappled with school and ran errands for the family. I was bound to live in a patient care facility, and Galtier Nursing in St. Paul was my first nursing home.

Galtier Nursing Home in St. Paul

According to relatives who attended on me, I was admitted into Regions Hospital Minnesota. After a few months, I was moved to Galtier Nursing Home in St. Paul in November 2013. Galtier provides intensive rehabilitation to help residents recover after surgery, an accident, cardiac event, or stroke, along with those seeking longer-term, skilled nursing care. They are dedicated to offer a wide continuum of health care services that balance the celebration of life with compassionate care.

I was admitted into Galtier because of memory lapses. The nursing aides complained about my disruptive and implicative behavior that slowed down work processes because cross teams were uncomfortably slow. Nursing aides couldn't catch up with other residents' support care plan scheduled simultaneously. To them, they always needed more time to complete their assigned tasks and skipped taking care of other desperate patients because of me. This attracted mild reproaches from their supervisors, which was cumulatively tantamount to corrective actions that might have tarnished their productivity and competence and jeopardized their jobs. They complained I was unruly, rude, sarcastic, and restless, and above all I demeaned their jobs.

Aides threatened to use sedative medications to subdue me. My wife threatened court action if that happened. Some occasionally neglected me and wouldn't clean excrement, emesis, and urine. A relative reported that he saw me on the veranda in one of the buildings without any aide coming to my assistance, and I urinated while trying to ask him with my manhood in hand. What I did in my confusion, I was astounded by the revelation. Thank God I am back to my brain with a sense of direction after miraculously defrosting all the medical injunctions and restrictions by God's grace.

Doctors confirmed that my memory had shrunk. My CT brain scan was similar to a seventy-six-year-old man at age forty-six in 2013, a discovery that made me thirty years older than my age. According to family care and personal attendants made up of close relatives and friends, doctors thought I needed serious neurosurgery of the brain to stabilize the disorder. Other medical authorities thought I would die, along with other nurses who believed I was in my last days.

My medical conditions deteriorated, and I developed an immune system disorder that ravaged my white blood cells to just one blood cell following a CD4 cell counts blood test. Due to a lack of funds, my wife solicited prayers from pastors and mosques. My wife pointed out, by God's mercy, I would one day meet them to offer a firm handshake.

That actually happened. One of the aides met me at a Target in Roseville and exclaimed "Chia!"

I am sure the Holy Spirit living in us urged my wife to spout out that assertion. How sweet is to know that God is my Father and I am his child, especially when the skies of my soul are cloudy and my cross weighs heavier. I always feel the need to repeat to Jesus that I believe in his love for me, especially when God's grace subdues insurmountable tribulations.

Immune System Disorder

Immune system disorders cause abnormally low activity or overactivity of the immune system. In cases of immune system overactivity, the body attacks and damages its own tissues (autoimmune diseases). Immune deficiency diseases decrease the body's ability to fight invaders, causing vulnerability to infections.

Think of white blood cells as your immunity cells. In a sense, they are continually at war. They flow through your bloodstream to battle viruses, bacteria, and other foreign invaders that threaten your health. When your body is in distress and a particular area is under attack, white blood cells rush in to help destroy the harmful substance and prevent illness.

In a situation in which my white blood cells were ravaged to just one white blood cell, death was imminent because my immune system was compromised by my immune system disorder, which ravaged my white blood cells and rendered me vulnerable to any infectious diseases. This meant that any disease and/or illness would exploit the vulnerability and could take my life. Those who attended on me intimated I was a living corpse because I lay in bed helpless and my illness deteriorated me almost to death. People who visited me at the hospital and nursing home said that each day passed in fear and they expected to hear of a death announcement because they didn't believe I would survive. Family members established their passports in readiness to travel to Cameroon in case I gave up the ghost. I actually kicked the bucket at some point because I stopped breathing for a few minutes. They gave up on me just to see my fingers activated to functionality. "Jesus said unto her, I am the resurrection, and the life: he that believeth in me, though he were dead, yet shall he live" (John 11:25 KJV).

Only God knows why I bounced back from death in my characteristic style, never giving up and looking forward. Thank you, Jesus. I am happy that, despite my traumatic illness, compounded by confusion, a nervous system breakdown, death, and resurrection, I am functional, even to a greater extent. My diabetes has improved, considering I am not more on insulin, which was injected by the day when I was a dweller in the nursing homes. My blood pressure looks good. I have regained my driving privileges and published a book, The Life of an African Peace Corps Child, and am now working on the one you are reading now, The Role of Divine Providence in My Life: Why I Am a Christian. My friends have nicknamed me "Miracle Man" due to my miraculous restoration of my health, my drivability, and all.

When I was still at the nursing home, guests to the Bethel Care Nursing Home who watched me descend into death and then resurrect myself continually greeted me with, "Welcome back." I couldn't figure out what they meant until one elder of the Presbyterian church of the way said, "Congratulations on your miraculous recovery. "You passed through the valley of the shadow of death." Psalm 23:4 (NIV)

I discerned that something wrong might have transpired with me that I was clueless about. Thank God you are reading from a one-time intense memory patient, demented in some circles and a corpse for few minutes and back to life. What do you think about God?

My illness was a mystery because the exact causes were unknown yet undiagnosed. This has been a huge challenge to the medical establishment because my situation has been enigmatic. The causes of my memory lapses flabbergasted doctors because it depleted my memory seriously to near zero and I regained itself without any neurological surgery and/or prescription. I guess God was the doctor.

When my primary doctor, Dr. Jarred Frandson, recommended a neuropsychology test, results showed that all six functions of my brain were damaged. Five were completely dead, and only one was marginal. Doctors have not ascertained the causes of my memory loss and rehabilitation. At first, a short-term memory test showed uncontrolled blood sugars mingled with my brain and led to confusion. They said a stroke shook my bodily function.

Now doctors consented it was a mild stroke that didn't manifest physically but shook my brain, leading to a complete breakdown of my body structure as I aged toward my mid-forties.

Body Coordination and the Human Nervous System Explained

Many scientists refer to body coordination as motor coordination, a term that describes the interactions between your muscular, skeletal, and nervous systems. Clear communication among these systems creates coordinated movements. Injury, disease, alcohol, drugs, and faulty postural alignment might cause communication roadblocks, which interfere with your body's ability to coordinate your movements.

When I did research to gain insight into what might have transpired in my illness, I discernibly believed that this shakedown of my bodily system might have caused my immune system disorder that triggered a breakdown of my nervous system. I believe that all these medical mysteries were a result of evil forces, and God performed his miracles.

When I was informally discharged from Galtier, my illness deteriorated, and I was rushed to the ER at Regions Hospital in St. Paul. While at home, I encountered episodes of confusion. Per my illness attendants, I occasionally rolled up one leg of my pants to my knee, put one sock on the other leg, and ran out in snow and very cold weather. My kids, Alan and Kaemia, ran out in an attempt to restrain me but couldn't succeed. They called in neighbors to help. I disturbed my kids and wife to the brink, and she called the police. I made a counter call that my wife had confined me in my house against my will. The police thought there was some form of abuse ongoing. Three police officers reported to our home with guns drawn. They questioned what was amiss, and those attending on me stated I was confused and restless. I disrupted the kids' studies and pursued my wife up and down the stairs. She couldn't sleep. The police asked which hospital I chose for emergencies, and I aptly chose Regions Hospital.

While at the aforementioned hospital, doctors and social workers advised that my wife should bring me to Bethel Care, a standard care center, so I could get courteous medical care. I checked into Bethel Care on February 11, 2014, and was discharged on May 31, 2015.

Bethel Care Center Nursing Home: My Fantasy World of Illusive Dreams

When I was a resident at the Bethel Care, there were two helpful nurses along with Jeremy, Paul and Lisa. Lisa, a nurse practitioner, recommended and prescribed many of my requisite medications. Occasionally at that center, I transitioned into a fantasy world of illusions. I visualized going to Cameroon in my imagination and returning to the United States. I actually thought I was in the house of my aunt, Mrs. Tubuo Senocia, at Banja Street, Nkwen, Bamenda, Cameroon, with whom I spent most of my adult life. Since I reported to the United States in 2003, I hadn't gone home to Cameroon and longed to do so. In my daydreaming, I told my family and friends that I needed to send money from Bamenda to my parents in Njinikom, Kom, about thirty-six miles away.

I reiterated my intention and hammered home the fact that, after I sent the money, I had plans to board a taxi thirty-six miles to Kom from the regional capital of Bamenda, where the governor resides. My friends pointed out that I was in Minnesota and wouldn't be able to travel as planned because I needed to board a flight to Europe, which took about eight hours. Transition wait time for the connecting flight would be six to seven hours. The connecting flight to Cameroon from Europe took another eight hours, making a total of about sixteen hours. They indicated that, if I added the net flight time to the transitional stopover time in Europe, I would be talking about twenty-one hours total to go to Cameroon. My people told me that going to Cameroon was an illusion because I was in a different country.

I almost fought with everybody around me at that time who injected accusatory language on me. They believed I was upright in my mind when I wasn't and chastised me for misspeaking. I told them that they were mad when I was the one suffocating with insanity.

When I was discharged from Bethel Care home, I discovered four boxes of diapers in the master's bedroom. Two diapers fell onto the bathroom floor. I turned around and asked my wife why she bought diapers and what for. She said they were mine.

I exclaimed, "Mine!"

She accepted. I asked what I used the diapers for. She elucidated an agonizing story, and I was overwhelmed with amazement. She pointed out that I encountered a breakdown in my bodily coordination and my human nervous system, which compounded my illness to an unbelievable proportion. I lost complete control of myself. I vomited, peed on myself, and pooped water, and I was completely out of my mind. I am told that I was very incoherent because information reached my sensory and short-term memory and disappeared in a flash

I attended a wedding of my friend, from planning committee, mass and reception but didn't know I did. When I regain my memory I visited their home and saw marriage photos on the wall. I asked when this happened and why I wasn't invited, I was told that I was there during the planning to the end. My wife had to take me because I was guided like a little baby. They said I was serious ill and that I am lucky because they made funeral arrangements contributing money. They said I was lost in thought because of cognitive impartment. I thank God for his faithfulness and mercy in my life considering what happed to my memory.

The cause(s) of my memory troubles and nervous system are still in a diagnostic stage, but I am almost 95 percent back to brain function, not by a lot of medication and/or surgery but by God's grace. I strongly believe that God was my biggest surgeon, and truly one of his incomprehensible miracles was yet to manifest in my recovery.

My memory issues deteriorated into a disability that required daily medical attention. Medical attention came with huge bills, and the burden was unbearable for my wife. She solicited advice from social workers on what to do to procure medical insurance for me. They asked about the intensity of the confusion, and she replied it was pretty serious and said she could ask my primary doctor to provide proof that the ailment was intense. The social worker advised that a proven mental or memory disability could mean procuring Social Security disability, which provided good benefits.

My wife contacted the Social Security disability office and got advice on the application formalities. I was scheduled to apply for benefits on July 2, 2013. They gave her a number of documents to submit on my behalf and stated why the application could be granted or refused. She applied and attached a strongly worded letter from Dr. Frandson, my primary doctor, to the Social Security disability office as testament of the intensity of my memory troubles. My Social Security disability application was granted on October 15, 2013.

Due to my disability status, my wife applied to the Ramsey County Department of Human Services for Medical Assistance, and it was granted. Medical Assistance (MA), Minnesota's Medicaid program, the largest of our state's publicly funded health care programs, works hand in glove with Social Security disability. MEDICA Insurance runs my medical plan. I schedule appointments in advance and use the MEDICA taxi services for transportation. The MEDICA taxi service uses five taxi agencies to move me back and forth. Taxis pick me up from my home to go to the medical facility of my choice.

Caring Professionals Homecare (PCA)

My PCA reports to work at our home at ten thirty in the morning and stops work at five after an eight-hour shift. She helps with cleaning, vacuuming, and dusting. She prompts me on activities, according to my care plan. She prepares and serves light lunches and provides my much-needed tea. This eliminates some kitchen work for my wife while she concentrates on her studies.

I am undergoing medical evaluation and assessment to restore my ability to work and drive. I visit a neurologist at the River Health Partners Clinic in Minneapolis. He has assessed and is working to repair my memory that was depleted when I fell sick. I make appointments with Fairview Uptown Clinic to meet Dr. Jarred Matthew Frandson, the primary doctor in charge of my diabetes; Carrie Fernandez, an occupational therapist who drills me on motor skills and administers neurologic tests; and Vicky Barth, an occupational therapist who, as a driving specialist, coaches me on driving rehabilitation skills. I practice driving on a simulator that replicates a real road situation. All these medical professionals are working diligently to get me back to normal life. I finally passed a doctor's recommended driving assessment and evaluation conducted by the most rigorous driving specialist at Regions Hospital Rehab Services.

Chapter 9

Peculiar Manifestation of Divine Providence and My Inclination to Christ in Prayers

When I made exploratory research on the role of divine providence on key American figures, I came across Reverend Martin Luther King Jr.'s most famous speech in 1963 that manifested in Barack Obama in 2008 when he ran for president of the United States.

When Reverend King made his most famous speech during the March on Washington in 1963, Barack Hussein Obama was two years and twenty-four days old. He was only six when Reverend King was assassinated in 1968. Despite the gap in their ages and the generational and geographical differences that helped define President Obama and Reverend King, their legacies are inextricably tied, albeit the president's legacy is still in the making. And since President Obama's nomination in 2008, there have been some momentous instances that, though coincidental, have connected the two men, happenstance that some of us have seen as divine providence.

Consider President Obama's acceptance speech for his party's nomination, made before eighty-four thousand people in a Denver football stadium. I was not the only one to note that it occurred on the forty-fifth anniversary of Reverend King's address telling America about a dream he had.

Then came President Obama's historic election, which had many in the country wondering if Reverend King could have imagined such a day. Ironically Robert F. Kennedy had predicted a couple months before Obama's birth that "in the next 30 or 40 years, a Negro can also achieve the same position that my brother has as President of the United States, certainly within that period of time."

Since I endured several tribulations during my childhood transition into adulthood and eventually made headway in life through divine providence, I made up my mind to implore the Holy Spirit to descend upon me to guide my livelihood.

I have committed myself to Jesus and his mother, Holy Mary. I pray the Holy Rosary twice a day, mornings and evening. I pray the Chaplet of Divine Mercy every day at three in the afternoon to beg God's mercy in all my undertaking, and this has changed my life to a larger extent.

Conclusion

My livelihood is inherent in divine providence. When I wrote The Life of an African Peace Corps Child, a book that recounts my childhood transition into adulthood, I reflected on my journey from early life into adulthood and discerned that a supernatural force steered my destiny. I thought that divine providential interventions propelled me toward achieving my utmost goals.

My place of birth is Cameroon, located in poverty-stricken sub-Saharan Africa. Being a Cameroonian was fateful because I was poor, and poverty revolved around my destiny in point and time. God providentially intervened to steer my future by orchestrating fateful happenstances that directed motion toward my growth process to achieve my utmost goals.

Everybody has his or her choices and priorities that influences one's destiny per God's design. God inserted himself into my future by transforming mishaps into celebratory achievements. If I missed one step, my story would never be mine. In this regard, a supernatural force orchestrated propelling coincidences of events that moved me forward in quest for a better life despite my pennilessness inherent in our family, showcased by my father's reluctance to work.

My bartender job fatefully earned a Peace Corps benefactor, Mr. Alan Lakomski, who sympathized with my neediness and sponsored my secondary education at age fifteen. He was an epitome of hope who set precedence on benevolent gestures and allowed destiny to take its course in my life. When he left unexpectedly, another heaven-sent Peace Corps volunteer, Bobe Bill Strassberger, came into my life when I encountered the ordeal of dropping out of school, an occurrence I detested because I did not have any alternative on the horizon for obvious reasons. He inculcated self-reliant skills, and I was able to support my education without any stand-alone sponsorship.

When I struggled through insurmountable difficulties to the University of Buea, I providentially connected with another fortunate Peace Corps benefactor, Dr. Christine Swanson, who supervised my end-of-course project and later encouraged me to apply to the University of Minnesota. She supported my visa search and provided lodging in her neighbor's house upon my arrival to the United States. Through her, I was lucky to reconnect to my original Peace Corps sponsors who forestalled the ordeal of homelessness and/or deportation. Both readily accepted to support me, as they had twenty-three years ago in Cameroon. Bill educated me on American culture, and Alan forestalled the threat of homelessness by providing me with financial support.

I now hold a master's degree of education in human resource development and am married with two kids. In 2013, I encountered a traumatic illness from memory lapses that almost took my life. My memory was compounded by a nervous system breakdown and immune system disorder that ravaged my white blood cells to just one. I reportedly died for a few minutes and was then resurrected. I believe it was God's orchestration to testify his goodness in my entire life. How do you feel?

The Bible says, "If [God] had not been there for me, [I never would have made it]. The minute I said, 'I'm slipping, I'm falling,' your love, God, took hold and held me" (Ps. 97:17 NIV). I never would have made it this far without God.

God is the best doctor, as he diagnosed my problems and divinely intervened in my life to solve them. He projected my selfhood and boosted my self-esteem. He restored my memory and nervous system and raised me back from death without surgery and no doctor's prescription. "If you listen carefully to the LORD your God and do what is right in his eyes, if you pay attention to his commands and keep all his decrees, I will not bring on you any of the diseases I brought on the Egyptians, for I am the LORD, who heals you" (Exod. 15:16 NIV).

I have committed myself to prayers by the day. Understanding the tribulations I endured and the positive hopes I nurse, I invested a lot of time on prayers, begging Holy Mary, mother of God, by praying the Holy Rosary and the Chaplet of Divine Mercy to implore mercy from Jesus to bless my undertakings. A change in my livelihood shows that God listens to my prayers and upholds my integrity in all facets of life.

Bibliography

Atkinson, R. C., and R. M. Shiffrin. "The Control of Short-Term Memory." Sci Am Scientific American 225(2): 82–90. doi:10.1038/scientificamerican0871-82.

Fukuda-Parr, S., K. Haq, and R. Jolly. "Editors' Introduction." Journal of Human Development 1(1): 7–8. doi:10.1080/14649880050008728.

Tasah, C. A. The Life of an African Peace Corps Child: The Life and Experiences of a Peace Corps Child of Kom, Cameroon. iUniverse, 2015.

"What is divine providence?" Accessed January 3, 2016. http://www.gotquestions.org/divine-providence.html.

"Genesis 1:27–28." Accessed February 2016. https://www.biblegateway.com/passage/?search=Genesis+1:27-28.

"Cameroon." http://www.nationsonline.org/oneworld/cameroon.htm.

"The Impact of Title II Regulation of Internet Providers On Their Capital Investments."

Accessed March 2016. http://www.sonecon.com/docs/studies/Impact_of_Title_II_Reg_on_Investment-Hassett-Shapiro-Nov-14-2014.pdf